THE SUMMARY OF THE GREAT VEHICLE

BDK English Tripiṭaka 46-III

THE SUMMARY OF THE GREAT VEHICLE

by

Bodhisattva Asaṅga

Translated from the Chinese of Paramārtha
(Taishō Volume 31, Number 1593)

by

John P. Keenan

Revised Second Edition

Numata Center
for Buddhist Translation and Research
2003

Revised Second Edition, First Printing, 2003
ISBN: 1-886439-21-4
Library of Congress Catalog Card Number: 2003111530

Published by
Numata Center for Buddhist Translation and Research
2620 Warring Street
Berkeley, California 94704

Printed in the United States of America

A Message on the Publication of the English Tripiṭaka

The Buddhist canon is said to contain eighty-four thousand different teachings. I believe that this is because the Buddha's basic approach was to prescribe a different treatment for every spiritual ailment, much as a doctor prescribes a different medicine for every medical ailment. Thus his teachings were always appropriate for the particular suffering individual and for the time at which the teaching was given, and over the ages not one of his prescriptions has failed to relieve the suffering to which it was addressed.

Ever since the Buddha's Great Demise over twenty-five hundred years ago, his message of wisdom and compassion has spread throughout the world. Yet no one has ever attempted to translate the entire Buddhist canon into English throughout the history of Japan. It is my greatest wish to see this done and to make the translations available to the many English-speaking people who have never had the opportunity to learn about the Buddha's teachings.

Of course, it would be impossible to translate all of the Buddha's eighty-four thousand teachings in a few years. I have, therefore, had one hundred thirty-nine of the scriptural texts in the prodigious Taishō edition of the Chinese Buddhist canon selected for inclusion in the First Series of this translation project.

It is in the nature of this undertaking that the results are bound to be criticized. Nonetheless, I am convinced that unless someone takes it upon himself or herself to initiate this project, it will never be done. At the same time, I hope that an improved, revised edition will appear in the future.

It is most gratifying that, thanks to the efforts of more than a hundred Buddhist scholars from the East and the West, this monumental project has finally gotten off the ground. May the rays of the Wisdom of the Compassionate One reach each and every person in the world.

NUMATA Yehan
Founder of the English
Tripiṭaka Project

August 7, 1991

Editorial Foreword

In January 1982, Dr. NUMATA Yehan, the founder of the Bukkyō Dendō Kyōkai (Society for the Promotion of Buddhism), decided to begin the monumental task of translating the complete Taishō edition of the Chinese Tripiṭaka (Buddhist canon) into the English language. Under his leadership, a special preparatory committee was organized in April 1982. By July of the same year, the Translation Committee of the English Tripiṭaka was officially convened.

The initial Committee consisted of the following members: (late) HANAYAMA Shōyū (Chairperson), BANDŌ Shōjun, ISHIGAMI Zennō, KAMATA Shigeo, KANAOKA Shūyū, MAYEDA Sengaku, NARA Yasuaki, SAYEKI Shinkō, (late) SHIOIRI Ryōtatsu, TAMARU Noriyoshi, (late) TAMURA Kwansei, URYŪZU Ryūshin, and YUYAMA Akira. Assistant members of the Committee were as follows: KANAZAWA Atsushi, WATANABE Shōgo, Rolf Giebel of New Zealand, and Rudy Smet of Belgium.

After holding planning meetings on a monthly basis, the Committee selected one hundred thirty-nine texts for the First Series of translations, an estimated one hundred printed volumes in all. The texts selected are not necessarily limited to those originally written in India but also include works written or composed in China and Japan. While the publication of the First Series proceeds, the texts for the Second Series will be selected from among the remaining works; this process will continue until all the texts, in Japanese as well as in Chinese, have been published.

Frankly speaking, it will take perhaps one hundred years or more to accomplish the English translation of the complete Chinese and Japanese texts, for they consist of thousands of works. Nevertheless, as Dr. NUMATA wished, it is the sincere hope of the Committee that this project will continue unto completion, even after all its present members have passed away.

It must be mentioned here that the final object of this project is not academic fulfillment but the transmission of the teaching of the

Buddha to the whole world in order to create harmony and peace among humankind. To that end, the translators have been asked to minimize the use of explanatory notes of the kind that are indispensable in academic texts, so that the attention of general readers will not be unduly distracted from the primary text. Also, a glossary of selected terms is appended to aid in understanding the text.

To my great regret, however, Dr. NUMATA passed away on May 5, 1994, at the age of ninety-seven, entrusting his son, Mr. NUMATA Toshihide, with the continuation and completion of the Translation Project. The Committee also lost its able and devoted Chairperson, Professor HANAYAMA Shōyū, on June 16, 1995, at the age of sixty-three. After these severe blows, the Committee elected me, Vice President of Musashino Women's College, to be the Chair in October 1995. The Committee has renewed its determination to carry out the noble intention of Dr. NUMATA, under the leadership of Mr. NUMATA Toshihide.

The present members of the Committee are MAYEDA Sengaku (Chairperson), BANDŌ Shōjun, ISHIGAMI Zennō, ICHISHIMA Shōshin, KANAOKA Shūyū, NARA Yasuaki, TAMARU Noriyoshi, URYŪZU Ryūshin, YUYAMA Akira, Kenneth K. Tanaka, WATANABE Shōgo, and assistant member YONEZAWA Yoshiyasu.

The Numata Center for Buddhist Translation and Research was established in November 1984, in Berkeley, California, U.S.A., to assist in the publication of the BDK English Tripiṭaka First Series. In December 1991, the Publication Committee was organized at the Numata Center, with Professor Philip Yampolsky as the Chairperson. To our sorrow, Professor Yampolsky passed away in July 1996. In February 1997, Dr. Kenneth K. Inada became Chair and served in that capacity until August 1999. The current Chair, Dr. Francis H. Cook, has been continuing the work since October 1999. All of the remaining texts will be published under the supervision of this Committee, in close cooperation with the Editorial Committee in Tokyo.

MAYEDA Sengaku
Chairperson
Editorial Committee of
the BDK English Tripiṭaka

Publisher's Foreword

The Publication Committee shares with the Editorial Committee the responsibility of realizing the vision of Dr. Yehan Numata, founder of Bukkyō Dendō Kyōkai, the Society for the Promotion of Buddhism. This vision is no less than to make the Buddha's teaching better known throughout the world, through the translation and publication in English of the entire collection of Buddhist texts compiled in the *Taishō Shinshū Daizōkyō,* published in Tokyo in the early part of the twentieth century. This huge task is expected to be carried out by several generations of translators and may take as long as a hundred years to complete. Ultimately, the entire canon will be available to anyone who can read English and who wishes to learn more about the teaching of the Buddha.

The present generation of staff members of the Publication Committee includes Marianne Dresser; Brian Nagata, president of the Numata Center for Buddhist Translation and Research, Berkeley, California; Eisho Nasu; and Reverend Kiyoshi Yamashita. The Publication Committee is headquartered at the Numata Center and, working in close cooperation with the Editorial Committee, is responsible for the usual tasks associated with preparing translations for publication.

In October 1999, I became the third chairperson of the Publication Committee, on the retirement of its very capable former chair, Dr. Kenneth K. Inada. The Committee is devoted to the advancement of the Buddha's teaching through the publication of excellent translations of the thousands of texts that make up the Buddhist canon.

Francis H. Cook
Chairperson
Publication Committee

Contents

Translator's Introduction

The *Summary of the Great Vehicle* (*Mahāyānasaṃgraha*) is perhaps the most representative text of the Yogācāra school of Mahayana Buddhism. Yogācāra, together with Mādhyamika, laid the foundation for subsequent Mahayana thinking. This text is a précis of Yogācāra philosophy on conscious interiority. Asaṅga (ca. 310–390), its author, is the principal thinker of this philosophic lineage. His work comes between earlier texts such as the *Scripture on the Explication of Underlying Meaning* (*Saṃdhinirmocana-sūtra,* Taishō No. 676; translated by John P. Keenan, Numata Center, 2000), the Maitreyan *Analysis of the Middle and the Extremes* (*Madhyānta-vibhāga*), and the *Ornament of the Scriptures of the Great Vehicle* (*Mahāyānasūtrālaṃkāra*), the source most frequently cited by Asaṅga in his *Summary* on the one hand and the later work of Vasubandhu and other commentators on the other.

The *Summary of the Great Vehicle* presents the classic argument for the basic Yogācāra themes on conscious interiority, attempting to reinterpret within this context the general Mahayana teachings of emptiness and dependent co-arising. The entire Yogācāra endeavor, it would appear, is aimed at evolving a critical understanding of consciousness that would ground the Prajñāpāramitā (and Mādhyamika) insistence on emptiness within a critically understood notion of the structure and functioning of conscious interiority. It then proceeds to explain the etiology of imaginative illusion, sketch its reversal by offering an explanation of the nature of conversion, champion the recovered insight into dependent co-arising in terms of the converted other-dependent pattern of consciousness, and thus allow for a valid, if limited, role for language-formed, conventional discourse, both commonsense and theoretical.

Chapter I launches into the program with a lengthy discourse on the structure of conscious interiority. It was evidently a felt need at the time of Asaṅga to go beyond logical attempts to deconstruct the illusion of essentialist thinking (Abhidharma) to an explication of the inner dynamic that results in both illusion and its reversal to wisdom. Consciousness is then presented not as a single inner knower looking out at external things but rather as a constant interplay between the latent container consciousness (*ālaya-vijñāna*), with all the defiled seeds (*bījas*) of past action, and the manifested, active consciousnesses of thinking, perceiving, and sensing, which bring to maturation those seeds and in turn plant new karmic seeds in the container consciousness—in an ongoing chicken-and-egg fashion for the duration of transmigration. Dependent co-arising denotes not only the interrelationships between things but also the structure of the mind itself, functioning as a synergy of these two levels of consciousness.

The *Summary* goes beyond the earlier *Scripture on the Explication of Underlying Meaning* in proffering the notion of the thinking consciousness (*manas*) as the locus of mistaking perceived images for realities. When converted, thinking also functions in interdependency between perceived images and insight; but in its initial appearance as defiled, images are mistaken for realities without any felt need for achieving insight into their meaning.

Chapter II moves to a discussion of the three patterns (*trisvabhāva*) in which consciousness functions. The most basic is the other-dependent pattern (*paratantra-svabhāva*), which, in a word, is the above structure of consciousness as co-arising in an interplay between the container and the active consciousnesses and in the interplay between image and insight in thinking. The imagined pattern (*parikalpita-svabhāva*) is the failure to understand this basic structure and the consequent clinging to things as if they had enduring essences. Frozen at the presentation of images as essences, one mistakenly affirms the reality of things that are in their very being empty and nonexistent. All things are empty inasmuch as all the ideas that are projected in the imagined pattern are without essence. The perfected pattern (*pariniṣpanna-svabhāva*), which Paramārtha renders as reality pattern, is the absence of imagining in the other-dependent pattern and the consequent recovery of its basic nature as other-dependent.

Chapter III treats the theme of conscious construction-only, the hallmark of Yogācāra. It is presented not as a subjective idealism, as has at times been thought, but as a rejection of the normative value of the subject-object polarity. Asaṅga reaffirms emptiness in teaching that in nonimaginative wisdom even the theory of conscious construction-only falls by the wayside, for it is only a conceptional and language-formed explanation and not itself insight into suchness.

Chapters IV to IX treat the development of the tyro bodhisattva through the perfections and stages to the full realization of wisdom. Chapter X turns to a treatment of wisdom as the three bodies (*trikāya*) of the Buddha, focusing in the main on the Dharma body (*dharmakāya*) so as to emphasize that this ultimate body is not a supernal essence floating off in some spiritual vacuum but is itself synonymous with emptiness as a nonimaginative awareness of suchness. The other two bodies, the enjoyment body (*saṃbhogakāya*) and the transformation body (*nirmāṇakāya*), are also drawn into this context, and Asaṅga insists that all Buddhas, whether seen in meditations in their pure lands or perceived as historical figures, are embodiments of emptiness and not objects to be clung to in mistaken devotion.

The *Summary* has five separate translations, one Tibetan and four Chinese, those by Buddhaśānta, Paramārtha, Dharmagupta, and Hsüan-tsang. The present English translation is taken from the Chinese translation of Paramārtha (499–569) made in 563. His translation is crucially important not only for deciphering the meaning of this most important Asaṅgan text but also in delineating the history of Chinese Buddhist thinking, for it led directly to the establishment of the Chinese She-lun Tsung (School of the *Summary*). Paramārtha did add passages to Asaṅga's text not found in any of the other translations, especially in reference to the theme of Buddha-nature. These added passages figure prominently in Chinese thinking on Yogācāra and on Buddha-nature.

There are two commentaries to the text: the *Commentary on the*

Summary of the Great Vehicle (*Mahāyānasaṃgraha-bhāṣya;* Taishō Nos. 1595, 1596, and 1597) by Asaṅga's younger brother Vasubandhu (ca. 320–400) and the *Interpretation of the Summary of the Great Vehicle* (*Mahāyānasaṃgrahopanibandhana;* Taishō No. 1598) by Asvabhāva (first half of the sixth century). Many passages yield their full meaning only when read in conjunction with these commentaries.

A preface is provided to the text by Hui-k'ai (517–568), who was a direct disciple of Paramārtha and worked as his amanuensis in writing down his interpretations and, truth be told, as his Chinese-language mentor. Hui-k'ai's preface is written in a somewhat florid style and is intended to recommend Paramārtha and his work to cultured Chinese gentlemen. Its Chinese is difficult and the English translation of it here is at times interpretive.

The numbering of paragraphs within the chapters is not present in the Chinese text but is taken from the French translation by Étienne Lamotte, one of the two Western-language works on the *Summary* available at the time of the first printing of this translation. Lamotte's *La Somme du Grand Véhicule d'Asaṅga* (*Mahāyānasaṃgraha*) 2 volumes (Louvain-la-Neuve: Institut Orientaliste, Université de Louvain, 1973), is based on the Tibetan text, and has long been the standard work on the *Summary.*

The Realm of Awakening: Chapter Ten of Asaṅga's Mahāyānasaṃgraha, translated by Paul Griffiths, Noriaki Hakamaya, John P. Keenan, and Paul L. Swanson (New York and Oxford: Oxford University Press, 1989), consists of an introduction to the thought of Chapter X together with a translation of this chapter of Asaṅga's basic text, of Asvabhāva's *Interpretation,* and of the three Chinese translations and one Tibetan translation of Vasubandhu's *Commentary.* It is meant to focus on the theme of Chapter X and to highlight the differences in translation in the commentarial literature.

In addition, Diana Paul's *Philosophy of Mind in Sixth-Century China: Paramārtha's "Evolution of Consciousness"* (Palo Alto, CA: Stanford University Press, 1984) presents the only book-length English-language study of Paramārtha and his thought. It is a well-researched and readable book.

At the time of publication of this revised second edition of the *Summary of the Great Vehicle,* an English translation of Gadjin M. Nagao's two-volume Japanese commentary, *Shōdaijōron: wayaku to chūkai,* is being done by Leslie Kawamura, John P. Keenan, Paul L. Swanson, and William S. Waldron. The breadth of Nagao's notes and the elegance of his explanations will make this work the new standard in English for scholarship on Asaṅga's *Mahāyānasaṃgraha*. It is a critical study that focuses on all the relevant materials: the Tibetan translation of Asaṅga's *Mahāyānasaṃgraha* and all four of its Chinese translations; and all translations of the two classical commentaries, Vasubandhu's *Mahāyānasaṃgraha-bhāṣya* (one Tibetan version translated by Dīpaṅkaraśrījñāna and three Chinese translations, by Hsüan-tsang, Dharmagupta, and Paramārtha), and Asvabhāva's *Mahāyānasaṃgrahopanibandhana* (one Tibetan translation by Jinamitra and one Chinese by Hsüan-tsang). Like the present translation, Nagao's enumeration of sections parallels Lamotte's for ease of cross-reference. When completed, this translation of Nagao's work will become the standard for the critical study of Asaṅga's basic text. By contrast, the present text addresses itself only to Paramārtha's Chinese translation of the *Mahāyānasaṃgraha,* and is not a comparative textual study, attempting only a faithful rendering of Paramārtha's Chinese.

THE SUMMARY OF THE GREAT VEHICLE

Preface to the *Summary of the Great Vehicle*

by Hui-k'ai

In a far-reaching manner, the excellent path is rich in insight, and 112b
in an impartial fashion its great compassion is conducive and inexhaustible. Its virtue encompasses living beings. Its truth is unbiased. Yet it is easy to embark on a wrong path, and bewildering illusions are difficult to allay. If one begins by discoursing on transcendence, then doubts cannot be eradicated. This is why [the Buddha] established the teaching and constructed the methods in accord with the character and disposition of sentient beings.

Before Yao and Shun, there were only a few simple guidelines, but after Chou of Chi there were many prolix rules and regulations. Although [rules] again and again regulated the ceremonies, proposed their instructions, and led the people by means of conventional teachings, the wondrous meaning of the true and the apparent remained hidden and unnoticed. Thus the progression [of the Buddha-Dharma] lay concealed west of the Pamir Mountains, and the teaching was hidden beyond the vast [East China] Sea. From the time when the House of Han (i.e., the Han dynasty) received the mandate, [that teaching] has slowly and gradually spread eastward until in the Chin dynasty it began to grow popular. When the Liang ruled the land, it prospered and became eminent. After about half a thousand years and seven generations [in China] it has come down to the present. Kumārajīva led [the people] forth to the pure source and spent his entire life in spreading its fragrance. Tao-an and Seng-jui, quickening [his] fertile ideas, developed it to its highest meaning. Tao-sheng and Seng-chao, searching out their mystic words, interpreted their deepest obscurities.

Whip in hand and loosening the reins, like the billows in a rapid torrent, [people] galloped off toward either the depths or the shallows and became confused about what is clear and what is obscure. Thenceforth, being excessively fervent and enthusiastic, none failed to run astray in their own directions. Their grasp of the teachings of the ancients and the practices of the patriarchs followed their own dispositions, and the opaqueness of their interpretations exceeded all limit.

In my heart I, Hui-k'ai, felt inadequate to assume the satchel [which contained the scriptures] (i.e., to take on the role of teacher), was embarrassed to gather my resources diligently, and [feared I might] lay out a mistaken direction for students and disciples. In sincerity I received instruction and, over a period of several years, visited innumerable places in order to study. Famous teachers were my dear friends, and I readily took their counsel. Yet in my investigations and inquiries I focused on the rustic and shallow without any hope of success. I examined the billows to trace out
112c the source, and there was much I did not understand. I hid this [lack of understanding], my thinking exhausted itself in the literal meaning of texts, and my notions were led astray from the broad meaning. I began the mornings with a sigh and frequently became dispirited. My entire attempt was to question the way according to current practice, yet I failed to see the path.

There was a Tripiṭaka master (Paramārtha) from the country of Ujjayanī. He was a brahman. His surname was Bhārata and his personal name was Kulanātha, which, translated, means "Savior of his Family." His discernment was profound and extensive. His visage was superior and his intelligence conspicuous. His eloquence was disciplined and far-reaching. His spiritual practice excelled the crowd, and his enunciation of virtue bypassed the common. When young he had visited all countries and studied under a succession of masters. He had initially studied non-Buddhist texts and fully understood the profundities of these books. He retained the four Vedas in his heart and the six kinds of Vedic commentaries in his innermost mind. He had also studied exhaustively the Three Collections (Tripiṭaka) of Buddhist texts. He thoroughly practiced the five classes of insight into the four truths and meditation. He examined the Great Vehicle and fully comprehended its deepest teachings. Dharma Master [Paramārtha] had made himself fully conversant with the ancient texts and discerned their subtleties. In all his desires he spread the wondrous truth in the border areas and elucidated the doctrine to those who had not yet understood. Committing himself to the path, he did not shrink from long journeys. He bestrode ten thousand miles as if they were a short stroll. He crossed the four seas as if they were small puddles.

In the second year of Liang-tai-ching he had just come to live in Chien-yeh, where he encountered the continual chaos at the end of the Liang. For this reason, the Dharma Master avoided the entire area, with the result that the great doctrine remained hidden and did not spread. Before he reached Chin-chiang, he turned back and went to Wu-ling. [At that time] he was not engaged in translating many scrolls, but when afterward he went to Min-yüeh, he preached frequently. The Dharma Master was magnanimous to all, his only lament being that there were few who understood his words. This is why Po-ya cut the strings of his lute [because after Chung Tzu-chi died, no one could appreciate his music] and why Pien-ho wept [tears of blood because his] jade [was thought to be false]. [Like Po-ya, Paramārtha] was skillful in the difficult interpretation of subtle passages. [As in the case of Pien-ho], the rarity of his wonderful jewel was exceptional. After a long period of traveling about, the Dharma Master desired to return to his native land. Retracing his steps along the highway, he came to Fan-yü. Ou-yang Wei, of sage visage and lofty spirit, who held the post of elder statesman (i.e., he held the ceremonial rank equal to the following three offices, without any specific duties), was magistrate of Hung-chou and prefect of Yang-shang and had become governor of Tung-ho. He was well versed in the classics and trained in military tactics. He supported the Way and aided the times, bringing peace to the homeless people in Pai-yüeh. He established the true doctrine in Wu-ling. He respected the noble conduct of the Dharma Master and honored his excellent discipline. Requesting that he become the Vinaya master, with full and due respect he observed the proprieties of a disciple.

I, [Hui-k'ai], had formerly received instruction and was in some slight degree purified, but the heavy dross [of illusion] lay hidden in my heart and for a short time I had withdrawn [from instruction]. Now I repeatedly honored and cherished [Dharma Master Paramārtha] and danced for joy. Once again I desired to feed on peace and true virtue. I inquired into the Way and expressed my doubts. Although I had been diligent, attentive, and earnest and was not slow-witted or recalcitrant, I had been irresolute and, losing the course, had not committed my heart.

The eldest son Ou-yang Ho, who was magistrate of Heng-chou and prefect of Yang-shang, was noble and moderate in his actions, dignified, upright, and well read in literature and history. In a profound and far-reaching manner he attended to the essentials of governing. He was a refined man of inner depth. His purity and brightness shone forth. He revered eminence and relished the path. He had genuine faith and loved the wonder [of the teaching]. Observing all the proper ceremonies, he personally made a request of my master. The Dharma Master was pleased to receive his request and agreed to engage in translation and interpretation [of the Buddha's teachings].

113a Dharma Master Hui-chih, abbot of Chih-chih Temple, was unsullied in his observance of discipline and totally engaged in spiritual practice. [Although] his mind was set upon quiet seclusion, when [something] ran counter to the path, he always rose to the occasion, inexhaustible in reforming and untiring in turning affairs around. Chung-ch'ing, the commandant of the Southern Army, was docile and intelligent in his progression in virtue. His resolution was simple and far-reaching. His excellent humor was pure and unadulterated, [sharp like] an icicle and evenhanded. He assisted in governing; and his fame quickly spread among the people. He deeply valued the Buddha-Dharma and cherished the highest truth. These two wise men, the monk [Hui-chih] and the officer [Chung-ch'ing], became [Paramārtha's] patrons.

With the sun shining each morning, the next year passed in harmony, and in the third month, when spring had arrived at

Chih-chih Temple, Dharma Master [Paramārtha] began his translation and interpretation [of the *Summary of the Great Vehicle*]. He already understood its grammar and had learned the [Chinese] dialect. All its words had to be elucidated and no meaning left imprecise or unclear. My teacher would sit on his mat until dawn without sleep. I, [Hui-k'ai], was his attentive scribe who copied down just what he said, word for word, phrase for phrase, chapter for chapter. Only after he had finished his examination [of the text] and translated its meaning did we issue the [Chinese] text. This translation was very difficult; and it could not be rendered in elegant Chinese. When there were variant readings, we reasoned out the differences and then were able to determine the basic meaning, for it is not permissible to issue a text with garbled meaning. Thus the present translation is a compromise between style and substance. We present it to the monks so that they may patiently study it together. If morning and evening they exert themselves without wasting an inch of the sundial, then, in the late spring of the year they begin, the text and its meaning will both be fully understood.

The basic text is in three scrolls, the *Commentary* in twelve scrolls, and the *Interpretation* in eight scrolls, which amount to twenty-three scrolls. This treatise is an outline of the Great Vehicle. The deep and wondrous meaning of the true doctrine arises cloudlike [from it], and its pure expressions overflow like the sea. It is both profound and far-reaching. Because of it the two vehicles fade into oblivion. Broad and formidable are its contents, which constitute the course of study on the ten stages.

About one thousand one hundred years after the departure of the Tathāgata, Bodhisattva Maitreya reached his appointed time, descended from his spirit abode, came down, and drew near. Forgetful of self, he deigned to respond to Dharma Master Asaṅga and to interpret extensively the meaning of the Great Vehicle. The name Asaṅga means "Nonattachment." The Dharma Master attained the unitary way and embodied its practice. He delved into the final limits of its mystery and made its spiritual reality

manifest. Because he wished to disseminate its excellent truth, he decided to write down this treatise. The language of conscious construction-only is subtle. But by following it one comes to understand and clarify the wondrous meaning of the three patterns. The elegant and abiding principles that it presents direct the course for sentient beings. The basic text was composed by Asaṅga. The Dharma Master's younger brother Vasubandhu, which, translated, means "Heavenly Friend," was born into the inferior way (i.e., the Hinayana) but in virtue he was endowed with the seed lineage [of the Great Vehicle]. His character was lofty and his spirit quick to discern. Having been prodded by his elder brother, he meditated on the broad meaning of the Great Vehicle. Recognizing that the style of all Master Asaṅga's treatises was profound and their meaning difficult to understand, he was concerned lest later students become confused. Therefore he composed his *Commentary* in order to interpret the basic text, in which he subsumed the lesser vehi-
113b cles and refuted heterodox teachings with the point of his brush.

From this point until the end of the second Period of the Counterfeit Dharma, the truly universal and perfect teaching flourished and spread. I, Hui-k'ai, do not regard [his efforts] as having been in vain. I feel concern that [sentient beings] will employ superficialities and try to sail their mustard-seed boats into the great sea. Thus I urge you to redouble your efforts to follow in the practice of the path. [This text] brought together anew all the smallest elements [of Asaṅga's teaching] to make a great bonfire and illumine sentient beings. By laboring over and carefully reading [the following text], the way of the illustrious gentlemen (*chün-tzu*) will not be lost.[1]

Introduction

The Chapter Titles of the Excellent Teaching on Support

1. This *Summary of the Great Vehicle* is an Abhidharma teaching on the scriptures of the Great Vehicle.[2] Standing before the World-honored One, Bodhisattva Mahāyānasupraviṇṭa, desiring to manifest the excellent qualities of the Great Vehicle, spoke in accord with the teaching of that Great Vehicle and said: "All World-honored Buddhas have ten excellent teachings, which are unequaled and unsurpassed by any other teachings."[3]

2. These ten teachings are 1) the excellent teaching on the support for the knowable, 2) the excellent teaching on the knowable, 3) the excellent teaching on entering into the knowable, 4) the excellent teaching on the cause and result of this entrance, 5) the excellent teaching on differences in the cultivation of the cause and result of this entrance, 6) the excellent teaching on the moral training that depends on these differences in cultivation, 7) the excellent teaching on the thought training that relies on this moral training, 8) the excellent teaching on the wisdom training that relies on this thought training, 9) the excellent teaching on abandonment as the result of this training, and 10) the excellent teaching on the differentiations of wisdom. The teaching enunciated by the Tathāgata surpasses other teachings. An interpretation of the scriptures such as this demonstrates that the truths of the Great Vehicle are the very words of the Buddha.

3. But how can the summary interpretation included herein demonstrate that the Great Vehicle is superior to other teachings? Because this summary interpretation treats ten themes that are found only in the Great Vehicle and not in the lesser vehicle.

What are these ten? They are 1) the container consciousness (*ālaya-vijñāna*) explained as the support for the knowable, 2) the three patterns of other-dependence (*paratantra*), imagination (*parikalpita*), and reality (*pariniṣpanna*) explained as the characteristic patterns of the knowable, 3) the doctrine of conscious construction-only (*vijñapti-mātratā*) explained as the entrance into the knowable, 4) the six perfections (*pāramitās*) explained as the causes and results of this entrance, 5) the ten bodhisattva stages (*bhūmis*) explained as the differences in the cultivation of these causes and results of this entrance, 6) the discipline (*śīla*) maintained and kept by bodhisattvas explained as the moral training
113c within these differences, 7) the concentrations (*samādhi*) such as those of the heroic march and the space storehouse explained as thought training, 8) nonimaginative wisdom (*prajñā*) explained as wisdom training, 9) non-abiding cessation explained as the resultant abandonment, and 10) the three Buddha bodies of essence (*dharmakāya*), reward (*saṃbhogakāya*), and transformation (*nirmāṇakāya*) explained as resultant nonimaginative wisdom.[4] Because these ten themes are found only in the Great Vehicle and differ from those of the lesser vehicle, we affirm that it is foremost. Because the World-honored Buddha has enunciated these ten themes for bodhisattvas, the ten excellent teachings of all World-honored Buddhas who rely on the Great Vehicle are affirmed to be superior to other teachings.

4. But how is it that the Great Vehicle with its unequaled presentation in the enunciation of these ten excellent teachings is the very word of the Tathāgata? How can one deny that the lesser vehicle is indeed also a great vehicle? Because these ten themes never appear in the lesser vehicle or in any of its interpretative commentaries but do appear in the Great Vehicle and are commented upon therein. Furthermore these ten themes are able to elicit the highest wisdom. They are valid, consistent, and logically cogent, so that sentient beings may attain a wisdom of universal understanding. We present verses:

The support of the knowable, its characteristic patterns,
Its entrance, its causes and results,
And the differences in cultivation,
The three trainings, and abandonment as result,
Together with wisdom are the sum of the Great Vehicle.
These ten themes are found nowhere else.
Gaining insight into them is the cause of wisdom.
Therefore the Great Vehicle is the Buddha's word,
Because he taught excellence in these ten themes.

5. Why are these ten themes presented in the above sequence? They are so presented because in their initial practices bodhisattvas must first examine the causes of all things just as they are, and in virtue of such an examination they must engender an intelligent understanding of the twelvefold dependent co-arising. Then they must understand and analyze the basic character of what is dependently co-arisen, through the understanding of which they can separate themselves from the two extreme mistakes of imputing being where nothing exists or subtracting being where it does exist. In this manner their correct meditation will penetrate to all the characteristics of objects just as they really are. Next they must become liberated from all obstacles. Having penetrated to the true characteristics of the knowable, by reliance on the purification of their inner aspirations they must bring the first six perfections, which they have already been cultivating, to completion and cause them to be purified without further defect. Then all the perfections comprised in that inner purification must be cultivated for three eons (*kalpas*) in the different conditions of the ten stages. Then the three bodhisattva trainings must be brought to fulfillment, after which the results of these trainings will be cessation (nirvana) and the supreme, highest awakening (*anuttara-samyak-saṃbodhi*). This is the sequence wherein they must attain these ten understandings through successive cultivations. The Great Vehicle attains its full plenitude in such a sequence.

Chapter I

The Support for the Knowable

Section 1: Characteristics

1. It is first explained that the support for the knowable is termed the container consciousness (*ālaya-vijñāna*). Where has the World-honored One spoken of this consciousness? Where did he call it the container? In the basic verses that summarize the Abhidharma, he said:

From beginningless time this realm 114a
Is the support for all things.
Only if it exists do all the destinies exist
And is there an access to cessation.[5]

2. Again in the Abhidharma another verse states:

The hidden ground upon which all things depend
Is consciousness with all its seeds (*bījas*).
Thus I call it the container
And have taught such for superior persons.

These two scriptural verses express the basic structure and the name of this consciousness.

3. Why did the Buddha teach that this consciousness is named the container? Because the results of the defiled mental states of all sentient beings lie concealed and stored up in it as results, and because this consciousness lies concealed and stored up in all those mental states as their cause. Furthermore it is called the container consciousness inasmuch as all sentient beings, clinging to an image of their selfhood, are themselves contained within [the confines of] this consciousness.

4. Scriptures, such as the following verse from the *Scripture on the Explication of Underlying Meaning* (*Saṃdhinirmocana Sutra*), treat the subject:

> The appropriating consciousness (*ādāna-vijñāna*) is deep and subtle
> Constantly flowing along with all the seeds of things.
> I have not taught this to common worldlings,
> Because they would reify it and cling to it as a self.[6]

5. Why does this verse speak of this consciousness as the appropriating consciousness? Because it appropriates and upholds all the physical sense organs of sentient beings and because it is the support for taking up all the experiences of rebirth. Why is this so? Because all the physical sense organs, having been appropriated by this consciousness, do not pass away until the end of life. When it continues into new rebirths, it is able to engender and make its own their formation, for this is how the physical bodies in the six destinies are appropriated. It is thus that the bodies in the six destinies are made one's own. Because this taking up is due to the appropriating of this consciousness, it is called the appropriating consciousness.

6. It is also called mind (*citta*), as the World-honored Buddha has spoken of mind, thought, and perception. Thinking is here of two kinds: 1) the immediately disappearing consciousness is thought because it is the condition for the subsequent thought, which arises in synergy with it, for we consider the support for the generation of consciousness to be thinking, and 2) defiled thinking is always yoked to the four passions of belief in selfhood, self-pride, self-love, and primal ignorance. This thinking is the support for the other defiled states of consciousness.

The other six defiled consciousnesses are engendered upon the support of the first kind of thinking and become defiled because of the second. The two are called thought (*manas*) because they objectify external things and are able to imagine sequentially (*manana*).

7. How can one demonstrate the existence of such a defiled mind? [There are six reasons:] 1) If this defiled state of mind did not exist, then solitary ignorance [unconnected with any other passion] would be impossible; 2) there would be no analogy with the five sense consciousnesses, for just as these five sense consciousnesses must have their own common, simultaneous support, that is, the five sense organs, [so defiled ideas and images must have their support in the defiled mind]; 3) the root meaning of the term "thinking" (*manana*) would be meaningless [if there were no defiled mind (*manas*)]; 4) there would be no difference between nonconceptual concentration and the concentration that destroys thought, for the defiled mind is present in nonconceptual concentration but not in mind-destroying concentration. If this were not their difference, they would be identical; 5) among unconscious gods [who have attained the above concentration], there would be no belief in self, self-pride, and so on, 114b
since they would be perfected in the absence of outflows, defects, and defilements; and 6) at all times the engendering of self-clinging occurs, in all good, evil, and morally neutral mental states. But if the defiled mind did not exist, then self-clinging and the illusions of self and its possessions could arise only with evil thought and not in good or neutral states. However, we avoid this error by allowing that the two minds [antecedent and defiled] arise simultaneously. But if one grants that illusions are activated solely in association with the six sense consciousnesses, one falls into this error.

> The absence of solitary ignorance; the analogy with the
> five sense consciousnesses;
> The identity between the two concentrations; the
> meaningless status for the root mind;
> The absence of self-clinging in states of no thinking
> during that period of concentration, which would
> issue in the absence of outflows;
> The nonarising of self-clinging in all good, evil, and
> neutral [mental] states.

If there were no defiled mind, the first two would not exist
and the latter three would be contradicted.
If it did not exist, then self-clinging would not arise
in all states.
Solitary ignorance is the illusory obstacle that causes
the realization of insight into true meaning not to arise,
and it occurs in all states.

Mind, although defiled, is comprised among morally undefined states, and it is always yoked to the four delusions. Being clouded and yet morally undefined, it is similar to the delusions in the worlds of form and formlessness, for the passions of these two worlds occlude quietude [although they are not morally evil either]. Such thought arises in each and every state without ceasing.

8. [Mind] does not refer to a third category apart from this container consciousness. Therefore the container consciousness comes to term in thinking and, dependent on it as seed, the other consciousnesses come to arise.

9. Why is this thought also called mind (*citta*)? Because it is a mental accumulation (*cita*) of the various seminal permeations.

10. Why did [the Buddha] not describe this mind by the terms "container" or "appropriation" in the word-hearers' vehicle? Because it belongs among the subtle objects of understanding. Word-hearers (*śrāvaka*s) are not expected to attain the preeminent wisdom of omniscience and thus, even though there is no mention of it among them, nevertheless their perfect [word-hearers'] wisdom leads them to fulfill their basic commitment. Thus it was not taught to them. But because all bodhisattvas are expected to attain the preeminent wisdom of omniscience, the Buddha taught it to them. Why? Apart from this wisdom, it is impossible to attain supreme awakening.[7]

11. Moreover the Tathāgata did present this consciousness in the word-hearers' vehicle, but in different terms. In the *Book of Gradual Sayings* (*Ekottarāgama-sūtra*) he stated: "People in the world love their possessions (*ālaya*), delight in their possessions, cherish their possessions, and are attached to their possessions."

It was in order to leave behind their possessions that the Tathāgata preached the true doctrine to them. It is because they were disposed to listen, give ear, pay attention, seek understanding, and 114c
engender true effort that they do leave behind and eradicate their possessions, for they put into practice the Tathāgata's true doctrine and follow it closely. It is because a Tathāgata appears in the world that such a singular, wondrous, inconceivable doctrine as that about the fundamental consciousness is manifested in the world. In this *Scripture on the Four Kinds of Good Qualities of the Tathāgata's Appearance in the World* (*Ju lai ch'u shih ssu chung kung te ching*) [from the *Book of Gradual Sayings,* we see that] this consciousness is already taught in the word-hearers' vehicle, although in different terms.

Moreover in a scripture of the Mahāsāṃghika school this consciousness is presented under the alternate term of "the foundational consciousness," for it is like the roots of a tree.

The Mahīśāsaka school also teaches this consciousness under an alternate name when it explains "the aggregate that perdures throughout transmigration." What does this mean? That although the continuity of material form and mind is at times severed, the seeds within the mind are not terminated.

12. Thus this container consciousness as the support for the knowable is already presented as a royal road in the lesser vehicle in the terms of appropriation, container, mind, the foundational consciousness, and the aggregate that perdures throughout transmigration.

13. Certain other masters hold to the opinion that the three terms—mind, thought, and sense consciousness—are synonymous. But this interpretation is incorrect. Inasmuch as it has already been admitted that thought and sense consciousness refer to different things, so one must understand [the term] mind also to refer to something different.

Yet other masters interpret the term "possessions" (*ālaya*) in the World-honored One's statement that "people in the world delight in their possessions" to refer to the five appropriated aggregates (*skandhas*). Yet others think that it refers to the sensations of enjoyment that accompany desire. Others think that it is clinging to a belief in selfhood. All these opinions are confused about this possession. When they draw their opinions from the scriptures and meditations, they do so in the context of the teachings and practices of the lesser vehicle and their proposals do not accord with true reason.

If they were not confused about the container consciousness, they would agree that our interpretation that these terms in the lesser vehicle refer to this consciousness is preferable.

Why is it preferable? [The term "possessions" does not refer to the appropriated aggregates because:] 1) Those who hold the opinion that possessions refer to the five appropriated aggregates should consider that for those born into one of the evil destinies filled with total pain, these appropriated aggregates are most detestable. It is not reasonable that those people would delight in such totally undelightful aggregates. Rather they constantly wish that those aggregates be severed and done away with. 2) It does not refer to the sensation of enjoyment that accompanies desire, since this sensation does not exist for those above the fourth meditation. If one had already experienced that sensation, then, when he seeks the higher realms, he will engender revulsion in its regard. Therefore it cannot be reasonably held that such persons delight in that sensation. 3) It cannot refer to belief in selfhood, because those within the true doctrine who believe in non-self negate such an attachment and engender no delight in it. Rather it is the container consciousness that is clung to as an inner self by the minds of sentient beings. Even if they are born into a destiny wherein they experience total suffering, their wish is only that that great mass of
115a suffering be obliterated and done away with, for they remain bound by self-love directed toward their container consciousness. They never wish or desire to eradicate their own selves.

Although those born above the fourth meditation never again delight in the pleasurable sensation associated with desire, yet they are still pursued by and not separated from their love of self in their container consciousnesses.

Likewise, those within the true doctrine, although committed to the doctrine of non-self and opposed to belief in selfhood, yet also have self-love for their container consciousnesses.

Thus this interpretation of the term "possessions" as signifying the [container] consciousness is preferable. Therefore this term is an alternate expression for the container consciousness.

Section 2: Characteristics

14. Here we treat the structural characteristics of this container consciousness, which in sum are three: its defining characteristic, its characteristic as cause, and its characteristic as result.

Its defining characteristic is that, relying on the permeations of all defiled states, it is the basic repository of seeds whereby the arising of those states is maintained. Its characteristic as cause means that this consciousness with all these seeds is the cause for the constant generation of those defiled states. Its characteristic as result means that this consciousness arises as the result of the beginningless permeations of these various defiled states.

15. What state is named permeation? What is the term permeation meant to signify? It is meant to signify the state, arising and passing away in tandem with those [defiled states], that is the generative cause for subsequent changes. It is like a sesame seed imbued with the fragrance of a flower. As the sesame and the flower's scent repeatedly arise and pass away in tandem, the sesame becomes the generative cause for that fragrance.

If a person engages in acts of lust, he becomes permeated with lust. As his mind repeatedly arises and passes away in tandem with lust, the lust becomes the generative cause for the [lustful] evolutions of his mind.

A scholar becomes permeated with learning. As his repeated acts of reflective listening arise and pass away in tandem with his thinking, that learning becomes the generative cause for his mind's understanding. Because this permeation becomes habitual, we say that such and such persons are learned in doctrine.

This same reasoning also applies in regard to the container consciousness.

16. Are these defiled seeds identical with or different from the container consciousness? They are not different as if they were separate realities. But, although when joined [to the container consciousness] they are not different from it, yet they are not identical with it either. The container consciousness arises in such a manner that when permeations are engendered, it has full capability to engender [defilements] as different. This is why it is called a seminal consciousness.

17. How is it that the container consciousness and these defiled states are simultaneously causes of one another? It is like the light and the wick of a lamp, for the arising of the light and the burning of the wick are simultaneous causes one of the other. It is also like a bundle of reeds that remain standing because [the reeds] simultaneously lean on one another.

Know then that the foundational consciousness and its per-
115b meations are reciprocal causes in a similar fashion, for this consciousness is the cause for defiled states and defiled states are the causes for this consciousness. Why is this so? Because no other cause can be found apart from these two.

18. How can permeation, which is not differentiated and not variegated, be the effective, generative cause for all things, which are differentiated and are variegated? It is like a garment woven with many threads; it does not have many colors but after it is put into the dyeing vat sundry patterns appear on its surface. In like fashion, at the moment when the container consciousness is permeated by a cluster of varied mental states, its one nature is not variegated. But when it is put into the dyeing vat of karmic results it takes on an incalculable variety of patterns.

19. Dependent co-arising as it appears in the container consciousness is the most subtle and most profound interpretation of dependent co-arising in the Great Vehicle.[8] In summary, there are two levels of dependent co-arising: that which distinguishes essences and that which distinguishes the pleasurable and the

unpleasurable. Dependent co-arising that distinguishes essences means that the arising of all things is supported upon the container consciousness, for it distinguishes the essences of the causes of all the varied things. That which distinguishes the pleasant and the unpleasant is the twelvefold dependent co-arising, for it distinguishes the various different causes for the pleasant and the unpleasant in good or evil destinies.

20. Those who are confused about the first dependent co-arising of the container consciousness imagine an original essence as the cause of transmigration, or think that past actions [create the present], or cling to the creative action of a creator god, or propose the self with its eight inherent qualities, or conversely claim that there is no cause at all.

Those who are confused about the second dependent co-arising imagine a self as the subject of action and experience. They are like the blind men who had never before encountered an elephant. When someone showed them one and had them feel it, some touched its trunk, some its tusk, some its ear, some its foot, some its tail, and some its flank. When asked what an elephant was, some of the blind men responded that it was like a plow handle, others that it was like a wooden pestle, a fan, a mortar, a broom, or a mountain rock. People do not understand these two kinds of dependent co-arising because they are blinded by primal ignorance. Whether they claim that the cause of transmigration is an original essence, past actions, the creative action of a god, the self with its eight inherent qualities, or that there is no cause, or whether they imagine a self as the subject of action and experience, because they do not understand the basic pattern of the container consciousness and its cause-result relationships, they are like those blind men who, not recognizing the shape of the elephant, offered such strange explanations.

21. In sum, the basic character of the container consciousness is maturing consciousness endowed with all its seeds. This consciousness is found in all persons in the three worlds and all the six destinies and four kinds of birth without exception.

22. As an aid to memory, this is presented in verses.

115c All seeds, external and internal,
Are undetermined in two points.
Whether provisional names or true realities,
All are characterized by six qualities:
Momentariness, simultaneity with results,
Sequential continuity,
A determined status, dependence on causes, and
Productivity of special results.

23. Stable, morally neutral, permeable, and yoked to the permeator—if unable to be otherwise permeated—this is the basic character of permeation. [These characteristics apply only to the container consciousness because] they are not associated with the six sense consciousnesses, because three [aspects of the six sense consciousnesses, i.e., support, object, and attention,] are different and opposed [to those of the container consciousness], because two moments are not simultaneous, and because one would then overextend the analogy [of permeation].

24. These external and internal seeds are causes that can bring things into being and maintain them. [For example,] they keep dried seed pods and corpses in being, for these things are destroyed only some time after [the initial causal force of the seeds has been removed].

25. [Although we spoke above about both external and internal seeds, one should be aware that] external seeds are different from internal seeds. Here are verses to explain this meaning:

External seeds do not permeate
[As when, for example, they are not planted],
But this is not the case with the internal seeds.
For it is unreasonable that
Without a permeation of learning
One should attain the result [of a learned mind],
And it is impossible that
What has been done should disappear or that
What has not been done should be realized.

It is in virtue of inner seeds that
The outer come to fruition.
Therefore it is the inner that permeate.

26. The other consciousnesses are different from the container consciousness. They are the active consciousnesses that are present in all births and destinies. Know that they are also called the experiential consciousnesses, as taught in a verse from the *Analysis of the Middle and the Extremes* (*Madyānta-vibhāga*):

The first is termed causal consciousness
And the second experiential consciousness,
Wherein the mental states of sense experience,
Discrimination of names, and activity take place.

27. These two consciousnesses are reciprocal causes one of the other, as a verse from the Mahayana Abhidharma states:

All mental states are stored within consciousness
And consciousness within all mental states.
These two are causes of each other,
As they are always results of each other.

28. If in the first dependent co-arising, all mental states [of the active consciousnesses] and [the container] consciousness are direct causes of each other, then in the second dependent co-arising, what kind of causality is exercised in regard to all these mental states? It is that of the dominant condition [of primal ignorance].

How many kinds of causality engender the six sense consciousnesses? There are three kinds of causality: dominant condition, object as cause, and immediately antecedent causality. They arise from these three kinds of causality, for [their dominant condition] is dependent arising within the limits of transmigration, their object as cause is the dependent arising in agreeable and disagreeable destinies, and [their immediately antecedent cause] is the dependent arising of the experiencing [of those destinies]. Thus [with their dominant condition being primal ignorance] four kinds of causality are involved.

Section 3: Demonstrations

116a 29. The container consciousness has now been demonstrated both in its various names and in its structural patterns. But how can one be certain that it is the container consciousness that is so described by the Tathāgata through these various names and in these structural patterns—that they do not also describe the active consciousnesses?

If the container consciousness were to be established apart from these names and patterns, then neither defiled nor purified states would be possible, for the defiled states of passion, action, and birth, as well as states of both worldly purification and world-transcendent purification, would not be possible.

30. Why would the defiled state of passion not be possible? Because it is impossible that the seminal permeations activated by the basic passions and the secondary passions come to term in the six sense consciousnesses. Why is this so? Let us consider the case where a visual consciousness arises and passes away in tandem with major or minor delusory passions of desire, and so on. It is this visual consciousness that becomes seeded by the permeations of delusory passions, not any other consciousness. Now after this visual consciousness has passed away, even if another [sense] consciousness intervenes, neither permeation nor a support for permeation can be found. The previous visual consciousness has disappeared and no longer exists, for it passes away and does not exist from the moment the other consciousness intervenes. It is then impossible for it to arise in tandem with existent desire, since a result cannot be engendered from an action that has been totally exhausted and has already passed away.

Furthermore, permeation does not occur in visual consciousness, even if it were to arise simultaneously with desire, and so on. Why? Because the seed does not dwell in the desire, since desire is supported by consciousness and because the continuity of desire is not stable.

Furthermore, desire in the other consciousnesses is not permeation, because their supports [which are the sense organs] are specific to each and because the other consciousnesses do not arise and pass away in tandem with each other.

[Visual consciousness does not permeate itself because two visual consciousnesses] of the same variety cannot permeate because they do not arise simultaneously in tandem with each other.

Therefore, visual consciousness is not permeated by the major or minor delusory passions of desire, and so on. It is not permeated by another consciousness of the same kind. This evaluation of visual consciousness also applies to the other sense consciousnesses.

31. Moreover, if a sentient being falls from the state of the unconcsious gods and is reborn into this lower world, then his consciousness from the instant of that rebirth is defiled by the major and minor delusory passions. But [if there were no container consciousness] his consciousness would at the time of rebirth lack seeds, for he would have already eliminated the permeations of delusory passions and their supporting [sense consciousnesses that support defilement].

32. Furthermore, when a countering consciousness has arisen then other worldly consciousnesses are eliminated. If there were no container consciousness, then this countering consciousness would arise in tandem with the seeds of the major and minor delusory passions, which is patently impossible. Why? Because its nature is liberative and because a mind without defiled outflows cannot arise and pass away simultaneously with delusory passions. Also, when after one emerges from insight into truth, [i.e., after the path of meditation that engenders the prior countering consciousness has passed into the path of vision,] and worldly consciousness arises, [if there were no container consciousness] then all the permeations of delusory passions would long since have been eliminated and a mental consciousness that had defiled outflows would arise without seeds [which is clearly impossible].

Therefore, the defilement of passion is impossible apart from the container consciousness.

33. Why is it that the defilement of action is not possible [in 116b
the absence of the container consciousness]? The member [of the

twelvefold dependent co-arising] "conditioned on karmic formations, consciousness arises" would be impossible, and it is unreasonable to say that "conditioned by appropriation, being arises" [if the appropriating container consciousness does not exist]. Therefore the defilement of action is impossible [if there is no container consciousness].

34. Why is the defilement of birth impossible [in the absence of the container consciousness]? Because there would be no link to a rebirth. When a person dies in a realm of nonconcentration [i.e., in the world of desire (*kāmadhātu*)], he comes to experience rebirth in virtue of a defiled thinking consciousness engendered in the entire intermediary state. When this defiled consciousness is eliminated in the intermediate state, then a consciousness formed in the embryo in the mother's womb experiences rebirth.

But if it is this thinking consciousness that becomes the support for the embryo, then within the mother's womb this thinking consciousness would engender another separate thinking consciousness, which cannot happen, since it is impossible for two kinds of thinking consciousness to arise simultaneously in the mother's womb.

Also, thinking consciousness cannot be the [consciousness] that formed in the embryo because thinking consciousness finds its support in defilement [while the womb consciousness is undefined], because it would always have an object [while thinking consciousness is at times interrupted], and because that object would be unknown [while the object of perceptive consciousness is known].

If it is this thinking consciousness that is formed in the embryo, then either the thinking consciousness formed in the embryo is itself the seminal consciousness or another consciousness arising upon the support of this consciousness is the seminal consciousness. If one holds the former, then it becomes identical with the container consciousness, simply being the same thing under a different name.

If one holds that another supported consciousness is the seminal consciousness, then thinking consciousness, because it is supported and caused by another, is a supported consciousness. But it is not reasonable to call it seminal if it is supported by another.

Therefore it is demonstrated that the consciousness that is formed in the embryo is not thinking consciousness but only the maturative and seminal [consciousness, i.e., the container consciousness].

35. Furthermore after a sentient being has been reborn it would be impossible for him to appropriate the material sense organs apart from the maturing consciousness. This is because the other sense consciousnesses all have their specific supports [in the sense organs] and because they are not stable. It is impossible to have sense organs without an appropriating consciousness.

36. Furthermore the mutual dependence between consciousness and the naming of perceptible things is like the mutual reliance of reeds standing in bundles and is impossible apart from the [container] consciousness.

37. Furthermore apart from the maturing consciousness there could be no mental sustenance for sentient beings who have already been born, because, apart from the maturing consciousness, not any of the consciousnesses of seeing, etc., have ever been seen to be able to sustain sentient beings born into the triple world.

38. If a person relinquishes this life and is reborn above in a land of concentration, it is in virtue of this scattered, defiled thinking consciousness that he experiences rebirth there. But apart from this maturing consciousness, it is impossible for that defiled, scattered mind to be the seed in that land of concentration.

39. Furthermore if a sentient being reborn into the world of 116c
formlessness (*arūpyadhātu*) engenders a defiled but morally good mind, then apart from the seminal, maturing consciousness it would be without seed and without support, thereby rendering impossible a mind both defiled and morally good.

40. If in the world of formlessness one engenders a mind without outflows then all other worldly states of mind are eliminated. [If then there were no maturing consciousness] then one would become extinct in that destiny.

41. If a sentient being in the destiny of neither conceptualization nor nonconceptualization engenders a mind of no outflows and

a mind of nonbeing then [in the absence of the container consciousness] he would immediately eliminate both these states, because that mind without outflows is a world-transcendent mind, and neither the destiny of neither conceptualization nor nonconceptualization nor the destiny of nonbeing nor the entry into cessation is its support.

42. Furthermore when a person who has performed good actions dies he becomes cold from his head downward. But a person who has done evil becomes cold from the feet upward, [for the former is moving to a higher destiny, but the latter to a lower one]. Apart from the container consciousness, this would not be possible.

Therefore apart from the seminal, maturing consciousness the defilement of birth is impossible.

43. Why is worldly purification not possible [if there is no container consciousness]? If a sentient being has not yet become freed from the world of desire with its cravings, if he has not yet attained a mind of the world of form (*rūpadhātu*), then he first engenders a good mind in the world of desire and strives to be freed from that world of desire with its cravings. But the thought of applying oneself to meditation is not permeated [by any mind of the world of form], because the thought of engaging in practice in the world of desire does not arise and pass away in tandem with any mind from the world of form. Therefore the good thoughts in the world of form are not the seeds for good thoughts of the world of desire.

Past states of mind in the world of form [from previous lives] have been eliminated by other states of mind through an unlimited number of other rebirths and thus they cannot act as the seed for subsequent states of concentration, because they do not exist.

Therefore it is demonstrated that the repeated influences of the seminal, maturing consciousness act as direct cause in regard to subsequent states of concentration in the world of form, while the good thought of engaging in practice acts as their dominant condition.

This explanation holds for all realms that are freed from desire. Thus apart from the seminal, maturing consciousness, states of worldly purification are impossible.

44. Why are world-transcendent states of purification impossible, apart from the container consciousness? The World-honored Buddha has taught: "True insight arises from hearing the voice of others and reflecting within oneself correctly." But this hearing of the voice of others and this correct reflection are unable to permeate the ear consciousness, or the thinking consciousness, or both together, [with seeds of transcendent purifications]. Why? When a person correctly reflects on the doctrine, as heard and understood, at that moment the ear consciousness is not operative. Furthermore that thinking consciousness also becomes inoperative when other distracting and discriminating ideas are heard. If this thinking consciousness that arises in tandem with correct reflection has long since disappeared, then the permeation of hearing with its permeating energy is already nonexistent. How then could such a no longer existent consciousness be the seed for the arising of a later consciousness?

Furthermore worldly thoughts associated with correct reflection never arise and pass away together with thoughts of world-transcendent purification, which are associated with true insight. There- 117a
fore these worldly thoughts are not permeated by those purified thoughts. Having no permeating energy, they cannot become the seed for world-transcendence.

Therefore apart from the seminal, maturing consciousness, the world-transcendent purified mind is also impossible, because the permeating energies of hearing and reflecting are unable to include the seeds of permeating energy for transcending the world.

45. How can this seminal, maturing consciousness, which is the cause for impure states of mind, bring about the countering of such defilement and be cause for the world-transcendent mind? The world-transcendent mind has never been experienced [by impure beings] and so it does not permeate their minds. If it does not permeate, then please explain from what cause does this world-transcendent mind arise?

The world-transcendent mind arises because its seed is the permeation of hearing that flows from the purest reality realm.[9]

46. Is this wisdom permeation of hearing identical with the container consciousness or not? If it is identical with the container consciousness, then how can it issue in the seed to counter this consciousness? If it is not identical, then where does this wisdom seed of hearing find its support?

Until the attainment of the highest awakening of Buddhas, this wisdom permeation of hearing arises in synergy with whatever supporting ground it abides in. Therein it arises together with the maturing consciousness, just as water [is mixed] with milk. But this permeation of hearing is not itself that foundational consciousness, for it is the seed that counters that consciousness.

47. Thus middle-level permeations arise by depending on lower states of permeation, while higher states depend on these middle states, because of [the progression of] hearing, reflection, and meditation cultivated repeatedly.

48. This permeation of hearing, whether lower, middle, or higher, is then the seed of the Dharma body (*dharmakāya*). Because it arises in countering the container consciousness, it is not comprised within that container consciousness. Since it is an outflow from the world-transcendent, most pure reality realm, even though a worldly state, it brings about the world-transcendent mind. Why? Because even when the world-transcendent purified mind has not yet arisen from this seed, all such superior states of mind counter delusory passions and all evil destinies. Furthermore they counter the decay consequent upon all evil actions, enabling one to maintain life continuity, thus favoring the encounter with all the Buddhas and bodhisattvas.

Although it is a worldly state, this permeation of hearing is comprised within the Dharma body as that which is to be attained by novice bodhisattvas, and in the liberation body as that which is to be attained by word-hearers and solitary enlightened ones (*pratyekabuddhas*). This permeation of hearing is not the container consciousness, for it is comprised within the Dharma body or the liberation body.

Thus as [this permeation] increases from small to middle to high, to the same degree the maturing consciousness decreases. The support is then converted. When that support is entirely converted, then the container consciousness with all its seeds is entirely eliminated together with all those seeds.

49. If this foundational consciousness arises and passes away 117b
in tandem with [the permeation of hearing that] is not the foundational consciousness, just as water is mixed with milk, then how can it be that the foundational consciousness is eliminated and that which is not the foundational consciousness is not eliminated?

It is just like the *haṃsa* (goose) that, when drinking, extracts milk from water. In a similar fashion, when worldly states are freed from desire, permeations from nonconcentrated realms are eliminated and permeations from states of concentration increase. This is how a worldly conversion of support becomes a world-transcendent conversion of support.

50. When one enters the concentration that destroys thought, it is not the maturing consciousness that leaves the body, for it has been taught that "consciousness does not leave the body." This is because the concentration that destroys thought is a countering not of this consciousness [but of the active consciousnesses].

51. How is this shown to be so? When one emerges from that concentration, there is no need for consciousness again to be engendered, for this maturing consciousness continues without interruption and, apart from the time of rebirth, need not be reengendered [upon emerging from any concentration].

52. Some persons say that the concentration that destroys thought does have thought. But this assertion cannot be demonstrated for the following reasons: because the meaning of this concentration would be lost; because [in this concentration] no recognition and no object can be established; because one would err [in implying] that this concentration is associated with good roots, since it is not associated with bad or morally neutral states; because one errs [in holding that] conceptualization and sensation arise

[therein] since then in concentration there would necessarily be contact and since it would have an ability to effect other concentrations (but the concentration of destruction is the obliteration of these); and because one errs [in holding that] such good roots as attention and faith arise [therein].

53. [If one tries to avoid the above errors by saying that the thought present in the concentration that destroys thought does not engage in mental activities, this can be refuted for the following reasons:] because one cannot validly remove the support from that which is supported; because there are examples [to this effect]; because the non-universal elements cannot be [separated from the universal] elements.

54. [Not present in Paramārtha.]

55. Some think that the sequential arising of form and mind is the seed of all beings, but this is not so, for not only does it involve the errors described above, but it has further separate misconceptions. These further mistakes are that in this opinion it would be impossible for one to fall from the abode of the unconscious gods or to emerge from the concentration that destroys thought, and that the last thought of a saint (arhat) would become impossible. If [that last thought] is apart from this sequence of causes, then this opinion is not valid.

56. Therefore apart from the seminal, maturing consciousness no purified or defiled states are possible. Therefore our interpretation of this mind is demonstrated and one must affirm and understand it as we have explained.

57. Here are verses:

When bodhisattvas abide in good mind,
They are freed from the five sense consciousnesses,
And without remainder their minds convert their supports.
By what other means could they do so?
Countering cannot be the conversion of support,
Because in abandonment it is absent.
One would then err in failing to distinguish

Cause from result in regard to abandonment.
The nonbeing of seeds or
Of their [seed-]natures [in the mind]
Cannot be the conversion of support,
Since, because they do not exist,
These two [alternatives] do not exist either, and
The meaning of conversion is impossible.

Section 4: Differentiations

58. What are the differentiations of this container consciousness? 117c
In sum there are three or four. There are the three different kinds of permeation: those of language, of belief in selfhood, and of the members of [the chain of] being.

59. There are also the four varieties: the projection of rebirth, its maturation, its referent, and its character. The projection of rebirth means that permeation arises anew, for if it did not it would be impossible for consciousness to arise conditionally upon karmic formations, or for being to arise conditioned upon appropriation. Its maturation means that in virtue of those karmic formations, those beings mature in the six destinies, for without this it would be impossible for any being who had experienced rebirth to be reborn at a later time. Its referent signifies that within the mind there is an image that engenders self-clinging, for without this, clinging to an image of self would be impossible. Its character means that this consciousness has a common character and a specific character, a seed-character as engendering the non-sensible and a seed-character as engendering the sensible.

60. Its common character is the seed of the physical world [that is common to all]. Its specific character is as the seed within each individual. Also its common character is as the seed for the engendering of the non-sensible and its specific character is as the seed for the engendering of the sensible.

When its counteragent arises, that which is countered and eliminated is its specific character, while true insight is purified, supported upon a consciousness of the common seeds and others' discriminations. It is just as a practitioner of meditation may take different attitudes toward the same object and as many ways of examining things as are established in accord with their mental [dispositions]. We present verses:

That which is difficult to eliminate and know
Is termed the common entanglements.
The thoughts of practitioners of meditation differ,
For the vastness of images forms the external world.
Even though [the external world] is not eliminated,
For purified persons therein insight is purified.
The perfection of the purified Buddha lands
Is due to the purity of Buddha insight.

Here is another verse:

It can be established that practitioners of meditation
Have sundry attitudes and insights
In regard to the same thing,
Because they are formed in accord
With their mental dispositions.
Because many insights are established,
That which is apprehended is conscious construction-only.

This foundational consciousness as specific is the seed for engendering a sensation of intelligent beings, for otherwise there would be no cause for the engendering of the sentient world. The common container consciousness as common is the seed for engendering the non-sensible [world], for otherwise there would be no cause for the arising of the physical, receptacle world.[10]

61. Furthermore there is a sluggish aspect and a lucid aspect to this [container] consciousness. Consciousness as sluggish refers to the seeds of the major and minor delusory passions. Consciousness as lucid refers to the seeds of all good states with outflows. If these
118a two were absent, one could not establish any difference between minds

that have superior capabilities and those that do not have superior capabilities, both of which are the results of previous actions.

Also there are two kinds of foundational consciousness: finished and not finished. Its character as finished is this consciousness as seed for the good and evil destinies that have already matured as results. Its character as not yet finished is its nature as the seed of language permeation, for from unlimited time it is the seed that engenders fabrication. Without this consciousness, the experience of the final, causal maturation of good or evil actions and omissions and the arising of new language permeations would both be impossible.

Furthermore it has a pattern of resemblance, for consciousness is like a magic trick, a mirage, a dream, or an optical illusion. This primary consciousness resembles these things. If this were not so, then this consciousness, as the seed for unreal imagining, could not be established as the cause of error.

Furthermore it is described as total and not total. It is total inasmuch as it is yoked to all the bonds of sentient beings. When one attains worldly liberation from desire, then that bondage is loosened. For adepts, word-hearers, and all the bodhisattvas, it is in part destroyed and eliminated, while for saints, solitary enlightened ones, and Tathāgatas, it is totally destroyed and eliminated. This is because saints and solitary enlightened ones have destroyed only the obstacle of delusory passion, while Tathāgatas have destroyed both the obstacle of delusory passion and the obstacle to wisdom. Without this [consciousness], this gradual destruction of passion would be impossible.

62. For what reason is [consciousness that] matures both good and evil states itself not occluded and not defined? There is no contradiction between the morally neutral nature [of the container consciousness] and the simultaneity of good and evil states. It is rather the good and evil that are in mutual opposition. If maturation itself were good or evil, then there would be no way to attain liberation from passion. And since there would be no

way to engender either goodness or passion, there could be no liberation and no bondage, for these two [qualities of being not occluded and not defined] would not exist. Therefore the maturing consciousness is certainly not occluded and not defined.

Chapter II

The Distinguishing Characteristics of the Knowable

Section 1

1. We have now explained the support for the knowable. What then are the distinguishing characteristics of the knowable? In sum they are three: the other-dependent pattern, the imagined pattern, and the reality pattern.

2. The other-dependent pattern consists of all the consciously constructed differentiations that have the foundational consciousness as their seed and that are included within unreal imagining. These differentiations are the conscious construction of the body, the conscious construction of the embodied person, the conscious construction of the experiencing person, the conscious construction of the content experienced, the conscious construction of valid experiencing, the conscious construction of time, the conscious construction of number, the conscious construction of place, the conscious construction of language, the conscious construction of a difference between oneself and others, and the conscious construction of being born and dying in good and evil destinies.

The conscious construction of the body, the embodied, and the experiencer, the experienced content, valid experiencing, time, number, place, and language are all engendered from the seminal permeation of language.[11] The conscious construction of the difference between oneself and others is engendered from the seminal permeation of belief in self. The conscious construction of being 118b
born and dying in good and evil destinies is engendered from the seminal permeation of the factors of existence. It is because such

conscious constructions are the salient features of other-dependence, found in the defilements of all worlds and destinies, that unreal imagining becomes manifested. These conscious constructs are comprised in unreal imagining, for they exist only as conscious constructs. The other-dependent pattern is the support whereby these nonexistent, unreal objects appear.

3. The imagined pattern is the appearance of nonexistent objects, which are only conscious constructs, as real.

4. The reality pattern is the eternal nonexistence in the other-dependent pattern of such objects and objective properties, for they have no existent reality.[12]

5. The conscious constructs of the body, the embodied, and the experiencer correspond to the six internal spheres of the sense organs. The conscious constructs that are the content of experience correspond to the six external sense spheres of perceptible objects. The conscious construction of valid experience corresponds to the six sense consciousnesses. The remaining conscious constructs are differentiations of these basic constructs.

6. Thus all conscious objects are only constructs of consciousness because there are no external objects. They are like a dream. In a dream everything is only a conscious construct without any relationship to any external object. All the objects that appear as real therein, such as the various material forms, voices, odors, tastes, touches, villas, gardens, lands, mountains, and so on, have no real objective being whatsoever. This example shows how in all cases there is only conscious construction. The term "and so on" above indicates other examples, such as magic tricks, mirages, optical illusions, and so forth.

Objection: You say that in all cases those things that are seen by a person who is awake are only conscious constructions like objects in a dream. But when a person awakens from a dream, he recognizes that the dreamed objects are only constructs of consciousness. Why then does one not similarly awaken from [the illusion of objectivity]?

Answer: It is similar, for a person who has attained a wisdom awakening to suchness does not lack such an understanding. Just as a person yet dreaming does not wake up as long as he remains dreaming, but a person already awakened does have this awareness. So one who has not yet attained an awakened wisdom to suchness lacks this awakening, but one who has already attained a wisdom awakening to suchness certainly has this awareness.

7. If one has not yet awakened to suchness in wisdom in regard to conscious construction-only, then how can he infer this understanding? He can do so by reflecting upon the scriptures and by true reasoning. In scriptures such as the *Scripture on the Ten Stages* (*Daśabhūmika-sūtra*) the World-honored Buddha taught, "Buddha sons, the three worlds are mind-only." And in the *Scripture on the Explication of Underlying Meaning* the great Bodhisattva Maitreya asked the World-honored Buddha, "World-honored One, are these images of things, which are the objects of the concentrated mind, different from mind or identical with mind?" The World-honored Buddha answered, "Maitreya, they are not different from mind, because I have taught that they are only conscious constructs. These images and objects of perceptible form are the appearances of conscious construction." Maitreya Bodhisattva then asked, "World-honored One, if these images of perceptible forms that are the content of the concentrated mind are not different from that concentrated mind, how can that consciousness apprehend those 118c
constructs as its objects?" The World-honored Buddha responded, "There is nothing that apprehends anything, yet although it cannot apprehend them, as the developments of this consciousness arise they appear in the guise [of those objects]. It is just as one sees on a mirror surface an image that appears to be different from that surface, while in fact he sees [only] the surface. In like fashion, that which appears in the concentrated mind seems to be objectively real, i.e., to differ from the concentrated mind [but in fact it is only a construct of that mind]."[13]

By reasoning upon this scripture we can clarify the meaning of conscious construction-only. How so? When the mind of a practitioner of meditation is already in the meditations of totality, he enters into a totality of color-image, as when he sees blue or yellow, but this mind does not itself see these material forms of blue or yellow as external objects. From this reasoning a bodhisattva can infer the meaning of conscious construction in regard to all consciousnesses.

8. The conscious construction of blue or yellow is not consciousness of memory, because the object seen is immediately present. In the mental consciousness of remembering what has been heard or reflected upon, consciousness has as its object things past, which arise as past. Therefore [this case of the concentrated mind] does demonstrate the meaning of conscious construction-only. From this inference a bodhisattva, even if he has not yet attained a wisdom awakening to suchness, can infer the meaning of conscious construction-only.

9. *Objection:* We grant that among the various conscious constructs explained above to be like magic tricks or dreams, those of the visual consciousness and so on are only conscious constructs. But how can this interpretation of conscious construction apply to material forms grasped by the eye consciousness?

Answer: As stated above, it can be understood both from scripture and from reasoning that these also are conscious constructs only.

Objection: If material forms are conscious constructs, then how do they appear as material? How do they perdure in solid homogeneity?

Answer: They do so because they are supported by the defilements, such as inverted thinking, etc. If this were not so, the inversion of taking as an object what is not an object would not occur. And if these two obstacles did not occur, then states of purification would not occur. Therefore, all conscious constructs are engendered in such fashion that they can be believed to be real. We present a verse:

The cause of confusion and confusion itself are
Constructs of material form and immaterial form.
If the first conscious construct did not exist,
The second conscious construct would not arise.

10. Why do the conscious constructs of the body, the embodied person, the experiencer, the content of experience, and valid experiencing come about in synergy and unison in all places of rebirth? Because they reach their term precisely in the experience of rebirth.

Why do the conscious constructs of time and the other differentiations treated above come about? Because the beginningless continuity of dying and being reborn is uninterrupted, [time arises]. Because the realm of sentient beings is incalculable, [number arises]. Because the environmental world is unlimited, [place arises]. Because the mutual communication of affairs is unlimited, [language arises]. Because the differentiations in appropriations and experiences are unlimited, [differentiations between self and others arise]. Because the maturations of actions, whether experienced as agreeable or disagreeable, are unlimited and because the differences in dying and being born thus realized are unlimited, [good and evil, their destinies, and the factors of existence arise].

11. What valid arguments establish these other conscious con- 119a
structs [i.e., the last six] as conscious constructs only? In sum there are three approaches: 1) since all constructs have been shown to be only conscious constructs, then the only criterion is conscious construction, for external objects have no existence; 2) there are only two components in conscious construction, i.e., image and insight; and 3) because the images variously produced are included in conscious construction.

What does this mean? Because all consciousnesses have no objects, we validate conscious construction-only as endowed with image and insight, for all sense consciousnesses have material form as their image and the sense consciousnesses as their insight, while the thinking consciousness has all the conscious constructs of sense perception as its image and thinking consciousness as its insight.

How can this be? Because the thinking consciousness is able to imagine and appear discriminately in the guise of all these conscious constructs. We present a verse:

> When practitioners of meditation who understand
> The single criterion,
> Its two components, and their varieties
> Reach an understanding of
> Conscious construction-only,
> They eradicate the standpoint of consciousness.

12. Some teachers say that, since in its arising the thinking consciousness takes different supports, it is referred to under different names, just as acts of volition are referred to as acts of body, speech, and so on, [inasmuch as they depend on the body, the voice, etc.] In all its various configurations engendered by its supports it appears as dual: as an external object and as the discrimination [of that object]. In all realms it appears as contact, but in form realms this thinking consciousness arises only in dependence on the support of the body. It is analogous to the material senses, which are also supported by the body. We present a verse:

> Those who have journeyed far and have journeyed alone,
> Bodiless and abiding in the cave of emptiness,
> Who have suppressed that which is difficult to suppress–
> They are liberated from the bondage of enmity.

As a scripture says:

> The thinking consciousness apprehends each of the objects of the five senses, for this thinking consciousness in its discrimination is their cause.

A further passage also says:

> When we describe discrimination,
> Among the twelve spheres [of sensation],
> The group of the six sense consciousnesses
> Is termed the thinking sphere.

13. When we here propose the foundational consciousness as the conscious constructor of objects, one must understand that herein all conscious constructs are termed the conscious construction of its image component, while the thinking consciousness and its supporting sense consciousnesses must be termed its conscious construction of the insight component. Why? Because conscious constructions of images are the supports that engender the activity of insight, since, being the cause for the occurrence of insight, they appear as external objects. This is how we establish that all conscious constructs are conscious construction-only.

14. How is it that, even though external objects appear before our eyes and are known, they do not exist? It is as the World-honored Buddha has taught, "When a bodhisattva attains the four understandings, he is able to comprehend and understand that all conscious constructs are without external object." What are these four? They are 1) the understanding that [the same object can] be the cause of contradictory conscious constructs, as when hungry ghosts (*pretas*), animals, and humans see different things in regard to the same object; 2) [the understanding that] conscious con- 119b
struction can occur from seeing what is not objective, as happens in regard to the past, the future, dreams, and fantasies; 3) understanding perfected spontaneously and unerringly, for, if an encounter with really existent objects produced conscious constructs, then there would be no point in any spontaneous and unerring understanding, since one would know them just as they are; and 4) the understanding that objects conform to the three wisdoms. What three wisdoms? They are 1) when wise persons enter concentration, they attain mastery over their minds, for at will they are masterful, and objects variously appear as intended; 2) when practitioners of concentration have attained quietude and turn their effort toward an examination of doctrine, objects appear in accord with their thought; and 3) when such persons have attained nonimaginative wisdom and have not emerged from nonimaginative concentration, no external objects appear at all. Because all objects conform to these three wisdoms and because

of the above-cited reasons for conscious construction-only, we conclude that only conscious construction exists and that external objects do not.

There are six verses that reiterate the above interpretation. Because these verses appear later in the chapter on wisdom training, they will be treated extensively there. They begin with the phrase, "Hungry ghosts, animals, humans...." [Chapter VIII, No. 20].

Section 2

15. If the support whereby what is only a conscious construction appears as an external object is termed the other-dependent pattern, how [in the absence of an external object as other] does it come to be dependent on others? Why is it said to be other-dependent? Because, arising from its own seminal permeation, it is interwoven with causes and cannot be independent [it is dependent on others]. Because it does not arise spontaneously and cannot even for an instant be independent, it is termed other-dependent.

If the imagined pattern is the other-dependent appearance of external objects as real, when they really do not exist, then how does it come to be imagined? Why is it termed imagined? Because the discriminations of thinking consciousness in unlimited ways cause error, it comes to be imagined. Because it has no specific character of its own, but is only the seeing of imagined distinctions, it is termed imagined.

If the reality pattern is characterized as the eternal absence of the imagined pattern, how does it come to be reality? Why is it termed reality? Because suchness is never not suchness, it is real-
119c ity. Because it perfectly purifies all realms and is the highest of all good states in the fullness of ultimate meaning, it is termed reality.

16. The imagined pattern is constituted by the presence of the act of imagining and something imagined. Here what state is referred to as imagining? What is that which is imagined? What is referred to as the imagined pattern?

Imagining is [the activity of] thinking consciousness, endowed with three kinds of imagining [of essences, shapes, and memories]. This consciousness [first as the imagining of essences and shapes] arises because its seeds are its own language permeations and the language permeations of all the sense consciousnesses. Because of its unlimited imagining in all places, it is termed the imagining [of memories]. That which is other-dependent is what is imagined. The imagined pattern refers to the basic activity of taking the other-dependent pattern as the content of imagining.

Why is this imagining able to fantasize upon the other-dependent pattern the images of the ten thousand things? What object does it encounter? Why does it apprehend these picture images? How does it see them and how does it dependently arise? How does it express itself in language and how does it increase? It names all its objects in the other-dependent pattern; it grasps images; it engenders seeing in judgmental categories; its intelligence dependently arises as presented in language; its four kinds of language about what is seen and so on affirm that which is actually without being to be existent and fantasize that which does exist to be nonexistent. Such is its activity of imagining.

17. Are these three patterns different from each other or identical with each other? They are neither different nor identical. One must explain them as [neither different nor identical]. In one specific sense, the other-dependent pattern is dependent on others. In another sense it becomes imagined, and in yet another specific sense it becomes reality.

In what sense is it termed other-dependent? In that it is bound to the other in its issuance from seminal permeation. In what sense does it become imagined? In that the other-dependent pattern is both the cause for imagining and that which is imagined. In what sense does it become reality? In that this other-dependent pattern, when it becomes reality, does not really exist as it was imagined.

Furthermore in what sense does this one [other-dependent] consciousness take on all the various configurations of consciousness? In that the conscious constructs that arise by virtue of both the fundamental consciousness and the other consciousnesses have these various configurations, and in that [these consciousnesses] arise because of those configurations.

18. How many varieties of the other-dependent pattern are there? In sum there are two. The first is that which occurs in tandem with seminal permeation, while the second is that which is unformed in regard to purification or defilement. Thus we speak of other-dependence in virtue of these two mutual relationships.

The imagined pattern is also of two varieties. The first is the imagining of essences, while the second is the imagining of specific qualities.

The reality pattern is also of two varieties. The first is essential perfection, while the second is purified perfection.

19. Furthermore imagination is also of four varieties. The first is the imagining of essences and the second is the imagining of specific qualities, while the third is that of intelligent persons and the fourth that of unintelligent persons. The intelligent are those persons who engender imagination from their ability to understand and differentiate names and words. The unintelligent are those who engender imagination with no such ability.

120a Moreover in yet another schema there are five varieties of imagination. The first is to imagine an essence in objects because of their names, as when one sees names as themselves implying objects. The second is to imagine an essence in names because of their objects, as when one takes objects to be intrinsic to names. The third is to imagine an essence in names because of those names, as when one imagines a name for a yet unknown object. The fourth is to imagine an essence in objects because of those objects, as when one imagines an object for a yet unknown name. The fifth is to imagine an essence in both names and objects because of both, as when one identifies names with objects and objects with names.

20. Or one can summarize all imaginings in ten varieties. The first is fundamental imagining, that is, the foundational consciousness. The second is imagining images, that is, the conscious constructs of perceptible forms. The third is imagining because of the appearing [of those images], that is, all the conscious constructs

of the sense consciousnesses, together with their supporting [images]. The fourth is imagining changes in those images, that is, the changes of old age and so forth, the changes of sensations of pain and pleasure, of lust and delusion, of oppressive times, or the changes of being reborn in the hells or in the world of desire. The fifth is imagining changes because of the appearing [of those images], that is, the arising of the changes described above. The sixth is imagining that is elicited by others, that is, the imagining that comes from hearing either false or true doctrine. The seventh is incorrect imagining, that is, the imagining of false doctrine of those outside the true doctrine. The eighth is correct imagining, that is, the imagining that comes from hearing the true doctrine of those within the true doctrine. The ninth is imagining that clings to its judgments, that is, the imaginings that arise in tandem with the sixty-two views that are based on belief in selfhood in all its varieties of incorrect reflection. The tenth is distracted imagining, that is, the ten kinds of imaginings of bodhisattvas.

21. The first of these ten distractions of bodhisattvas is distraction through an image of nonbeing. The second is distraction through an image of being. The third is distraction through imputing being to what is not. The fourth is distraction through negating being to what is. The fifth is distraction through clinging to unity. The sixth is distraction through clinging to differentiation. The seventh is distraction about totality. The eighth is distraction about specific qualities. The ninth is distraction that takes objects to correspond to names. The tenth is distraction that takes names to correspond to objects.

22. In order to counter these ten kinds of distracting imaginings, the World-honored One has taught in all the Perfection of Wisdom (Prajñāpāramitā) teachings that nonimaginative wisdom is able to counter these ten distractions. Thus one should recognize that the full significance of the Perfection of Wisdom scriptures lies in how the bodhisattva is to practice these perfections of wisdom in accord with the explanation of those scriptures. They teach, "Śāriputra, a bodhisattva is indeed a bodhisattva" [in order to

counter the image of nonbeing]. They teach, "One does not see an existent bodhisattva" [in order to counter the image of being]. They teach, "One does not see the name bodhisattva, the perfection of wisdom, practice or the absence of practice, perceptible form, sensation, conceptualization, volitional dispositions, or consciousness, for the essence of form is empty" [in order to counter the imputation of being to what is not]. They teach, "They are not empty because of that emptiness" [in order to counter the negation of that which is]. They teach, "That emptiness within perceptible forms is not identical with those forms" [in order to counter the clinging to unity]. They teach, "No form is differentiated from emptiness" [in order to counter clinging to differentiation] for "form is emptiness and emptiness is form." They teach, "This is because, Śāriputra, these are only names" [in order to counter the distraction about totality]. They teach, "That which is referred to as the essence of
120b form neither arises nor passes away and is neither defiled nor purified [in order to counter distractions about specific qualities]. They teach, "It is through artificially established names that one imagines all beings" [in order to counter the mistaken correspondence between objects and names]; that "Things are as they are because they follow upon language, which artificially establishes their incidental names" and "People engender sundry attachments because of such language constructs" [in order to counter the mistaken correspondence between names and objects]. They teach, "Of such names none are seen by the bodhisattva, who consequently engenders no attachment," for if he should take note of the aggregates, he would also elicit this reflection.

From these passages from the Perfection of Wisdom scriptures one should accordingly reflect upon the meaning of the ten distractions.[14]

23. If in this sense the other-dependent pattern comes to be in all three patterns, then how can there be three patterns? How can these three different patterns not become commingled? There is no commingling because of the principle that, when this pattern becomes other-dependent, it does not thereby become either imagined or

reality; that when it becomes imagined, it does not thereby become other-dependent or reality; and that when it becomes reality, it does not thereby become either other-dependent or imagined.

24. But how does one know that when the other-dependent pattern appears as the imagined pattern, it is not identical with that imagined pattern? Because it is contradictory that any substance to things be intrinsic to its name, since prior to the acquisition of names no understanding arises in regard to objects, and many names would indicate many objects, but this is contradictory. It is also contradictory that since names are undetermined, objects should also be disunified substances. We present verses on this:

> There is no understanding prior to naming;
> Names are many and indeterminate.
> It is contradictory for objects to be
> Identical with substances, to be many, or to be disunified.
> The nonbeing of beings appears as being.
> The undefiled yet becomes purified.
> Thus it is like a magic trick,
> Like the empty sky.

25. Since the other-dependent pattern does not really exist as it appears, how does one know that it is not entirely nonexistent? If there were no other-dependent pattern, then the reality pattern would also be nonexistent, and one would then come to affirm universal nothingness. And then, if the other-dependent pattern and the reality pattern both did not exist, one would fall into error about the being and nonbeing of defilement and purification. But since these states can be known not to be nothing, it is not true that all is nothing. We present a verse:

> If there is no other-dependent pattern,
> Then the reality pattern also does not exist.
> Then there could never be the two states
> Of defilement and purification.

26. All the World-honored Buddhas have preached the broad

scriptures of the Great Vehicle, wherein it is asked: How should
120c one understand the imagined pattern? It should be understood through the teaching that such states do not exist.

How should one understand the other-dependent pattern? It should be understood through the teaching on such similes as a magic trick, a mirage, a dream trace, a shadow, a reflection, a valley echo, the moon in water, a transformation.

How should one understand the reality pattern? It should be understood through the teaching on the four kinds of pure states. These are 1) original, essential purity, that is, suchness, emptiness, the reality limit, the imageless, reality, the reality realm; 2) undefiled purity, that is, the above state separated from all adventitious obstacles; 3) the purity of the path whereby one reaches that [undefiled purity], that is, all the factors favorable to awakening, all the perfections, and so on; and 4) the purity of the object that engenders that path, that is, the truly enunciated doctrine of the Great Vehicle. Why? Because this teaching is the cause for purification, it is not imagined. Because it is an outflow from the pure reality realm, it is not other-dependent. These four pure states encompass all pure states without exception. We present a verse:

> Such similes as magic refer to the other-dependent.
> The teaching of nonbeing refers to the imagined.
> The teaching of the four purities treats reality.
> These purities are the origin, the undefiled,
> The path, and the object.
> All pure states are encompassed in these four.[15]

27. Why and wherefore is the other-dependent pattern explained in the scriptures through similes such as the magic trick and so on? In order to eliminate the delusions and doubts of others about the other-dependent pattern.

How can these others be shown that their doubts about the other-dependent pattern are unjustified? In order to resolve the doubts of those who say, "If there really are no things, then how can one validate the objective world?", it is taught that it is like a magic trick.

In order to resolve the doubts of those who say, "If there really are no objects, then how can the mind and its activities arise?", it is taught that it is like a mirage.

In order to resolve the doubts of those who say, "If there really are no external things, then how can one experience pleasure or pain?", it is taught that it is like a dream trace.

In order to resolve the doubts of those who say, "If there really are no beings, how can good or evil actions produce pleasant or unpleasant results?", it is taught that it is like a shadow.

In order to resolve the doubts of those who say, "If there really are no beings, then how do the various understandings arise?", it is taught that it is like a reflection.

In order to resolve the doubts of those who say, "If there really are no beings, then how can language arise?", it is taught that it is like a valley echo.

In order to resolve the doubts of those who say, "If there really are no beings, then how can one actually encounter real beings as objects of the concentrated mind?", it is taught that it is like the moon in water.

In order to resolve the doubts of those who say, "If there really are no beings, then how could bodhisattvas resolve unerringly to experience birth in the six destinies to benefit others?", it is taught that it is like a transformation.

28. With what intention did the World-honored One say in the *Scripture of Brahmā's Questions* (*P'o lo men wen ching*) that a Tathāgata sees neither the cycle of birth and death (samsara) nor cessation? His underlying intention was to teach the undifferen- 121a
tiation whereby the cycle of birth and death is cessation because they are grounded within the other-dependent pattern [respectively] as the imagined and reality patterns. This is because the other-dependent pattern in its imagined aspect becomes the cycle of birth and death and in its reality aspect becomes cessation.

29. In the *Abhidharma Scripture* (*Abhidharma-mahāyāna-sūtra*), the World-honored One taught three aspects: 1) the defiled aspect, 2) the pure aspect, and 3) the defiled and pure aspect.

What was his intention in teaching these three aspects? While the defiled aspect is the imagined pattern within the other-dependent pattern, and the pure aspect is the reality pattern within the other-dependent pattern, the defiled and pure aspect is the other-dependent pattern itself. This was his intention in teaching these three aspects.

What analogies can be offered for his intention? It is like a lump of gold with three aspects: elemental earth, gold, and a lump of soil. In the elemental earth, a lump of soil is visible, although it does not exist [for it is really gold], while the gold, which does really exist, is not visible. But when the lump of soil is heated in the furnace, then the previously invisible gold appears. When the lump of soil appeared as the elemental earth, this was an illusory appearance. But when the gold appears, this is the appearance of reality. Thus the elemental earth has two aspects.

In a similar way, when the fundamental consciousness has not yet been heated in the furnace of nonimaginative wisdom, this consciousness appears as the unreal, imagined pattern, and the reality pattern does not appear. But when it is heated in the furnace of nonimaginative wisdom, this consciousness appears as the perfected, reality pattern, and the unreal, imagined pattern does not appear.

Therefore the consciousness of unreal imagination, that is, the other-dependent pattern, has two aspects. It is like the primal matter that contains gold covered over by dirt.

30. Furthermore in certain passages the World-honored One taught that all things are eternal; in other passages, that all things are transient; and in yet other passages, that they are neither eternal nor transient. This was his intention in teaching the eternal, transient, and neither eternal nor transient natures of all things.

This same interpretation holds for suffering, pleasure, and the absence of either; for good, evil, and the absence of either; for emptiness, nonemptiness, and the absence of either; for self, non-self, and the absence of either; for quiescence, nonquiescence, and the absence of either; for essence, non-essence, and the absence of either; for arising, nonarising, and the absence of either; for passing away, no passing away, and the absence of either; for original quiescence, no original quiescence, and the absence of either; for original cessation, no original cessation, and the absence of either; for the cycle of birth and death, cessation, and the absence of either.

One should interpret the underlying intent of all the distinctions taught by all Buddha Tathāgatas by following the structure of the three patterns as above. We present verses:[16]

As things have no reality,
And as they appear in various ways,
He explained their nonduality 121b
As neither reality nor unreality.
From a single perspective he taught
Either being or nonbeing;
From a double perspective he taught
Neither being nor nonbeing.
Beings are not as they appear;
Thus he taught their eternal nonbeing.
But beings actually do exist in their appearances;
Thus he taught their absence of nonbeing.
Because substances do not of themselves exist,
Because substances do not of themselves perdure,
Because they do not exist as apprehended,
The three patterns validate the three absences of essence.
Because of non-essences,
One establishes their momentary basis,
Their original quiescence as neither arising nor passing away,
And their original cessation.

31. Furthermore, the teachings of all World-honored Buddhas should be interpreted according to their four intentions and four aims.

The four intentions are 1) the intention to make an identification, as for example when it is taught that "At that time I was called Vipaśyin, who had attained Buddhahood"; 2) the intention to declare a future event, as for example when it is taught that "If a person recites and bears in mind the name of Bahuratna Buddha, he is assured of attaining supreme awakening without ever again falling back," or when it is taught that "Only those who have elicited the vow to be born in the Buddha Land of Bliss will be born there"; 3) the intention of indirect reference, as for example when it is taught that "One can attain full comprehension of the Great Vehicle by serving Buddhas as numerous as the sands of the Ganges River"; and 4) the intention to accord with the dispositions of sentient beings, as for example when the Tathāgata first effusively praised the charity of a certain person and then afterward severely censured it [in another person]. As with charity, the same applies to discipline and the other perfections. These are termed the four intentions.

The four aims are 1) the aim of causing one to enter, as when in the great or lesser vehicles the World-honored Buddha taught the conventional truths that identify the general and specific characteristics of persons and things; 2) the aim of disclosing patterns, as when he taught that the three patterns necessarily exist in the teaching on the specific nature of things; 3) the aim of countering, as when the practices that counter the eighty-four thousand passionate actions of sentient beings are clarified; and 4) the aim of interpreting, as when a meaning different from the literal sense is expressed in order to elucidate a different meaning. An example of this is found in the following verse: "Those who take the unsubstantial for the substantial, who are well established in error, who are afflicted by all the passions—they attain supreme awakening."

32. If one desires to interpret the overall doctrine of the Great Vehicle in summary, he should treat the three themes: 1) he should elucidate the character of dependent co-arising, 2) he should elucidate the true character of dependently co-arisen states of being, and 3) he should elucidate the meaning of what has been taught [in the scriptures in light of the above two].

The elucidation of the character of dependent co-arising is as the verse declares, "All things arise from the permeations of language and these [permeations] from those [things]," that is, the maturing consciousness and the actively evolving consciousnesses are causes one of the other. 121c

The elucidation of the true character of dependently co-arisen states of being means that the nature of all things, being characterized as active evolutions of consciousness, is conscious construction endowed with image and insight. Furthermore all states of being are characterized as support, imagined, and reality. In these words the nature of all states of being is elucidated within the context of the three patterns. We present a verse:

> Issuing from that which has both image and insight,
> One knows that all states of being have the three patterns.

How can one elucidate the characters of these states? Within the other-dependent pattern, the imagined pattern lacks any reality whereby it might exist, but the true reality pattern really does exist therein. It is in virtue of this nonbeing and this being that at the same time spontaneously perfected suchness is realized or not, seen already or not yet seen. For in the other-dependent pattern, the imagined pattern does not exist, but the true reality pattern does exist. If one sees one, one does not see the other. We present a verse:

> In the other-dependent, the imagined does not exist,
> But true reality does exist.
> Therefore the absence of realization and realization
> Are both equally present in it.

The elucidation of what has been taught consists of explaining and analyzing texts that have previously been taught [by the Buddha] in the light of later commentaries, whether concerning the assemblage of good qualities [of the Buddha] or the various aims of practice [of bodhisattvas].[17]

33. The body of good qualities, which is an elucidation of the World-honored Buddha's good qualities [as presented in the scriptures], consists of the purest wisdom: 1) his nondual action, 2) his unmarked state of being the highest refuge, 3) his arrival at the

Buddha abode, 4) his realization of equality with all Buddhas, 5) his attainment of unhindered activity, 6) his unerring and unopposable doctrine, 7) his unchanging sphere, 8) his inconceivable establishment of doctrine, 9) his equality in regard to the three times, 10) his manifestation of bodies in all world realms, 11) his unhindered wisdom in all things, 12) his wisdom joined with all his practices, 13) his wisdom without doubt in regard to all things, 14) his unimaginable bodies, 15) his wisdom as that which is to be experienced by all bodhisattvas, 16) the perfection of his nondual Buddha abode, 17) his attainment of the undifferentiated liberation wisdom of a Tathāgata, 18) the finality of his attainment of equality in all Buddha lands, 19) the ultimacy of his reality realm, and 20) his extension to the limit of the realm of empty space.

Just as the initial phrase "purest wisdom" is interpreted later by the commentarial explanations, so one must in turn distinguish and interpret each of the following phrases.

If one would correctly explain the meaning of the doctrine, he must expand upon "the purest wisdom" by explaining that the wisdom of the Buddhas and Tathāgatas is pure and without misunderstanding in regard to all things. In this basic meaning are comprised all twenty-one good qualities: 1) the quality of arising without any obstacle to knowledge whatsoever; 2) the quality of causing
122a entrance into the highest purity of true suchness without duality in regard to being and nonbeing; 3) the quality of the Buddha abode wherein the Tathāgata's activity is effortless and uninterrupted; 4) the quality of the absence of differentiation in support, intention, and action in the Dharma body; 5) the quality of countering all obstacles to practice; 6) the quality of suppressing all heretical doctrines; 7) the quality of arising in the world without being defiled by worldly states; 8) the quality of true doctrine validly established; 9) the quality of responding to the questions of others through the four skillful answers; 10) the quality of manifesting enjoyment bodies in all world realms; 11) the quality of resolving the doubts of others; 12) the quality of introducing others to various practices; 13) the quality of understanding the arising of future things; 14)

the quality of manifestation in accord with the aspirations of sentient beings; 15) the quality of taming sentient beings by the true doctrine through convening unlimited assemblies; 16) the quality of the fullness of perfection of the equal Dharma body; 17) the quality of manifesting pure Buddha lands in accord with the aspirations of sentient beings; 18) the quality of the inseparability and undifferentiation of the three Buddha bodies; 19) the quality of engendering benefit and gladness for all sentient beings to the limit of the cycle of birth and death; and 20) the quality of inexhaustibility.

34. "The various aims of practice" are expressed in the scripture as, "If a bodhisattva has thirty-two qualities, he is called a bodhisattva." They embrace the intention to bestow benefit and gladness upon sentient beings: 1) their intention to lead sentient beings to enter the wisdom of omniscience; 2) their wisdom to accord with their present situations; 3) their abandonment of pride; 4) the firmness of their good intentions; 5) their intention of being benevolent without simulation, of not currying favor, of being [equally] impartial to friend and foe, and of always being good teachers until they enter final cessation; 6) their quality of speaking in good measure and gently, smiling before beginning to talk; 7) their compassion for all sentient beings without differentiation; 8) their not faltering or growing fainthearted in carrying out their tasks; 9) their quality of not becoming bored; 10) their quality of never being satiated with hearing doctrine; 11) their quality of confessing their own faults, while disregarding and not censuring the faults of others; 12) their quality of maintaining an awakened mind in all their deportment; 13) their quality of practicing disinterested charity, of not displaying fear in any destiny, of maintaining discipline, of being unerringly patient to all sentient beings, of zealously engendering all good states and practices, of cultivating contemplation, except those of the world of formlessness, and their wisdom joined to skillful means (*upāya*), that is, yoked to the four enticements; 14) their quality of being good friends to both the disciplined and the undisciplined without distinction, of being respectful in serving good teachers, of being respectful in

hearing doctrine, of enjoying dwelling in forest places, of not being fond of worldly fads, of taking no joy in the lesser vehicle, of appreciating the Great Vehicle, and of avoiding evil friends and respecting and serving good friends; 15) their quality of constantly maintaining the four Brahmā abodes, of maintaining unlimited purity
122b of mind, of sporting in the five supernatural powers and taking refuge in wisdom; and 16) their quality of not abandoning people of either proper or improper conduct, but including everybody, of speaking in a definitive manner, of revering truth, and of prioritizing and respecting action.

The word "bodhisattva" is associated with these states. The above phrases have been taught [in the scriptures]. The interpretation through later [commentaries] means that "their intention to benefit and gladden sentient beings" is elucidated through sixteen descriptions of bodhisattva practice, which are 1) their continuous practice; 2) their unmistaken practice; 3) their personally initiated practice; 4) their indestructible practice; 5) their disinterested practice, which interprets the three phrases about their not currying favor, not being attached to or repulsed from attractive or unattractive sentient beings, and continually practicing in later lives; 6) their practice of speaking in accord with circumstances, which interprets the two phrases about speaking and smiling; 7) their impartial practice in regard to sentient beings, whether suffering, happy, or neither; 8) their practice of not denigrating others; 9) their practice of not retrogressing; 10) their practice of skillful means of enticement; 11) their practice of destroying what must be countered, which interprets the two phrases about their own and others' faults; 12) their practice of uninterrupted deliberation; 13) their practice of cultivating excellence, which interprets the seven phrases about true meditation and intense practice of the six perfections and the four enticements that are done respectfully; 14) their practice of perfected skillful means, which interprets the six phrases about service to good teachers, hearing true doctrine, dwelling in forest places, avoiding perverse thoughts, true reflection, which covers two phrases, and associating with good friends, which is expressed in two phrases; 15) their practice of perfection, which interprets the three phrases about maintaining the immeasurable with purity of mind, the practice of august powers, and the realization of good qualities; and 16) their practice of establishing others, which covers four phrases about convening assemblies, proclaiming and teaching doctrine without hesitancy, gathering together offerings according to the doctrine, and the undefiled mind.

Through these commentarial explanations we have interpreted the previous passages. Here is a verse:

> When one takes up the previous phrases,
> They are analyzed as a sequence of good qualities.
> When one takes up the previous passages,
> Each is analyzed in light of its intention.

Chapter III

Entry into the Distinguishing Characteristics of the Knowable

1. Having explained the distinguishing characteristics of the knowable, how are we to understand the distinguishing characteristics of entry into the knowable?

[That entry] is supported by the permeations of much hearing [of the doctrine of the Great Vehicle] and is not comprised within the container consciousness. Rather, just as [occurs] with that container consciousness, so [this permeation] is a seed that develops [within consciousness]. It is comprised in correct reflection.[18] [Such correct reflection in turn] arises from images that appear as doctrine and its meaning. [These images] are discriminated in mental words that are accompanied by insight and that appear as if connected to apprehended [realities].

2. Who enters into the characteristics of the knowable? All [bodhisattvas] who have permeated the continuities [of their con- 122c
sciousnesses] with much hearing of the Great Vehicle, who have already rendered service to all the innumerable Buddhas who appear in the world, who have already entered a true state of definitive commitment, and who, through well-matured meditation, have increased their good roots and thus accumulated the two stores of merit and wisdom.

3. At what points [in their development] do these bodhisattvas gain insight into conscious construction-only? In virtue of a discrimination of the images and mental words accompanied by insight that appear as doctrine and its meaning, and in virtue of the arising of insight into the doctrine of the Great Vehicle, they enter the state of practicing earnest commitment upon firmly believing

what they have heard; they enter the path of insight upon intelligently understanding [what they have heard]; they enter the path of meditation upon countering all obstacles [to that insight]; and they enter the final path upon going beyond obstructing defilement to the utmost purification. The reality of all things exists only as conscious construction as [just] explained, in virtue of an earnest commitment to what is heard, of an intelligent understanding, of a countering of all obstacles, and of a going beyond obstructing defilement to utmost purification.

4. Why do they come so to enter? Because they are supported by the force of good roots; because they have sharpened their minds in three aspects; because they have eradicated the four basic barriers; and because, with uninterrupted and reverent meditation upon the doctrine and its meaning in quietude and insight, they have not been distracted.

5. The first sharpening of their minds [is expressed in the following thought]: "Innumerable and immeasurable sentient beings in the human realm—since world realms in the ten directions are innumerable and immeasurable—from moment to moment realize supreme awakening."

The second sharpening of their minds [is expressed in the thought that] "In virtue of correct intentions [of sentient beings] the perfections of giving and so forth inexorably mature. I too have committed myself and attained such stability and, in virtue of my correct intention, will without difficulty progress in the cultivation of the perfections of giving and so forth and attain their fullness."

The third sharpening of their minds [is expressed in the thought that] "Persons with good mental states after death in all their rebirths effortlessly attain pleasant and joyful destinies, for they have attained a limited goodness. Even with their limited goodness these persons still come to such attainments. How then would I who have achieved perfect and unlimited goodness not come to attain pleasant and joyful destinies at will?"

Here stanzas refer [to these three sharpenings]:

Sentient beings in the human realm
Realize awakening at each and every moment
In places beyond reckoning.
Thus let not your mind be downcast.

The commitment of good persons enables them
To engender the perfections of giving and so forth.
Since the Victors attain these dispositions,
They are enabled to cultivate giving and so forth.

When good persons die, they attain superior joy.
How then would not those whose purified goodness
In its perfection eliminates [all] gradations
Be lacking in these accomplishments?

6. They eradicate the four barriers: 1) because they abandon the thoughts of word-hearers and solitary enlightened ones, perverse 123a
notions are destroyed; 2) because they engender a mind of faith in and clear understanding of the Great Vehicle, they destroy all perverse ideas and doubts; 3) because they abandon perverse attachments to "I" and "mine" in regard to the doctrine they have heard and reflected upon, they destroy attachment to doctrine; and 4) because thoughts about images standing over against [their minds] are not discriminated, they are able to eradicate discrimination.

Herein a stanza states:

Because the wise do not discriminate
Thoughts about all the images
That appear and stand before [them],
They attain supreme awakening.

7. How and by what means do they come to full understanding concerning doctrine and its meaning?

[They so understand] because of the discrimination of mental words accompanied by insight that are linked to the permeation of hearing, that are comprised in correct reflection, and that appear as doctrine and its meaning.

[They so understand] because of the four inquiries on the designations of names, objects, essences, and differences.

[They so understand] because of the four reality wisdoms, for in these four kinds of reality wisdoms names, objects, essences, and differences do not exist.

When entering into the understanding of these things, bodhisattvas zealously endeavor to gain insight into conscious construction-only through the appearance of the mental words involved in such insight, which appear as written words and meanings to be discriminated. They fully comprehend that the images of those written words are merely the discriminations of mental words, that objects, depending on names and words, are merely discriminations of mental words, and that such names, objects, essences, and differences are valid only as conventional designations.

Then at this stage, upon realizing that they are only the discriminations of mental words, these practitioners of meditation see that designations are neither names nor objects, neither essences nor differences, since in their real character there are no objective essences or differences.

Thus they gain insight into conscious construction-only through the four inquiries and the four reality wisdoms that bear upon the names and objects that appear in the discrimination of mental words.

8. What state is entered in understanding conscious construction-only? What is it like?

One enters a state of cognition-only, a state of duality of image and insight, and a state of multiplicity. Since the six images of names as essences, differences, and designations, and of objects as essences, differences, and designations, have no objectivity [one enters a state of cognition-only].

Because of the subject and object structure, which also lacks objectivity, [one enters a state of duality].

Because many apparently different patterns of things do appear simultaneously, [one enters a state of multiplicity].

It is just as in the dark a rope might appear to be a snake, while in fact that snake is an illusion and does not exist in the rope. Thus when people have clearly examined the objective rope, their previously confused awareness of a snake is [seen] to be without objective foundation and falls away while only the rope is known to be present. Yet this knowledge of the rope, when subtly analyzed, is also chimerical and without objective foundation, because it is characterized by material form, odor, taste, and contact, [none 123b
of which have any stable and objective foundation]. When the mind encounters these objects, its knowledge of the rope is also negated. When with a parallel insight one eradicates the apparent names and objects that appear in these six images, then discriminative, defiled understanding in mental words will no longer arise, just as in the knowledge of the snake. In suppressing objectivity in these six images, just as was the case with the knowledge of the rope, by relying on the wisdom of suchness the understanding of conscious construction-only itself can be rejected.

9. In this fashion, in understanding that the images discriminated by the mental words appear as objective, the bodhisattva fully understands the imagined pattern. In understanding the meaning of conscious construction-only, he fully understands the other-dependent pattern. But how does he understand the reality pattern?

By abandoning any idea about conscious construction-only! At that moment the bodhisattva clearly understands the imagining of mental words, which long since had been yoked to the permeations of hearing doctrine, and he suppresses any idea of their correspondence with the external world. These [ideas] no longer arise because their apparent objective status no longer has any cause and thus they do not even arise as an imagining of the mental words of conscious construction-only. This implies that the bodhisattva dwells only in nonimagination in regard to all objects and names, and in virtue of nonimaginative wisdom he realizes and abides in the reality realm of suchness. He then enters the reality pattern because of the arising of nonimaginative wisdom wherein subject and object are entirely identical.[19]

10. Herein a stanza states:

Things and persons, texts and meanings,
Statements both concise and extended,
Beings defiled and purified, and the final stage—
These ten are the different spheres of naming.

11. Because the bodhisattva has gained insight into conscious construction-only, he has attained understanding of the characteristics of the knowable. Through fully understanding these characteristics, he has attained entry into the first stage of joy, well penetrated into the reality realm, attained birth in the lineage of all Buddhas in the ten directions, and attained impartiality in thinking about all sentient beings, bodhisattvas, and Buddhas. This is termed the bodhisattva's path of insight.

12. Why does the bodhisattva once again become aware of conscious construction-only?

Through a transcendent wisdom of quietude and insight focused on the all-pervading doctrine and through a wisdom characterized by a variety of images and conscious constructs attained subsequent to nonimaginative wisdom, he eradicates all the causal seeds in his fundamental container consciousness and nurtures all the seeds that enable one to contact the Dharma body. He converts his support and comes to attain the true qualities of all Tathāgatas, and he attains the wisdom of omniscience. This is why he [again] becomes aware of conscious construction-only.

Seeing magical illusions in all the constructs that arise from the container consciousness and all the images of those imagined constructs, that wisdom attained subsequently to nonimaginative
123c wisdom is fundamentally exempt from error. Just as a magician is himself undeceived by his magic tricks, so the bodhisattva, when enunciating the path of cause and result, always remains free from error in all his descriptions.

13. When one truly gains understanding of conscious construction-only, there are four concentrations that support the good

roots of the four aids to penetration. How should a bodhisattva understand this?

Through the four inquiries during the inferior efforts at recognizing the absence of objectivity, the concentration of the acquisition of clarity supports good roots for aid to the penetration of fervor.

In superior efforts at recognizing the absence of objectivity, the concentration of increased clarity supports the good roots for aid to the penetration of crowning practice.

In the four reality wisdoms, when the bodhisattva has gained insight into conscious construction-only and clearly understands the absence of objectivity, the concentration of partially penetrating reality supports recognition that is well-disposed toward truth not mediated through language.

Immediately following this concentration, the clear suppression of the idea of conscious construction-only becomes an uninterrupted concentration that supports the highest worldly state.

These four concentrations are methods whereby bodhisattvas gain insight into and bring to presence the truth not mediated through language.

14. When the bodhisattva enters the first stage, he has attained the path of insight and acquires full understanding of conscious construction-only. But how does he practice meditation? How does he enter into the path of meditation?

He attains [the stage of] presence as described in the teachings in the extensive discourses of the Buddha on the ten bodhisattva stages, which summarize the twelvefold scripture of the Great Vehicle taught by all Tathāgatas, because he masters both the general and the specific [meaning of doctrine] since he engenders transcendent, nonimaginative wisdom that focuses on the far-reaching universal import [of doctrine] and a wisdom of quietude and insight acquired subsequently to that nonimaginative wisdom [which focuses on specific doctrinal meanings]; because for immeasurable and incalculable millions of eons he relies on these many practices of meditation; because, by virtue of his conversions of support both previously and presently attained, he intensifies his meditative practices in order to bring about an attainment of the three Buddha bodies.

15. What are the differences in the path of insight of word-hearers and bodhisattvas?

There are eleven differences herein: 1) a difference of object in that the object for a bodhisattva is the doctrine of the Great Vehicle; 2) a difference of support in that his support is the store of great merit and wisdom; 3) a difference in penetration in that he penetrates the non-self of both persons and things; 4) a difference in cessation in that he reposes upon non-abiding cessation as his abode; 5) a difference in stages in that he relies on the ten stages for liberation; 6) and 7) a difference in purification in that he both destroys the permeation of passion and brings pure lands to purity; 8) a difference in impartiality of mind in regard to sentient beings in that, in order to mature sentient beings, he does not discard
124a effort in relation to their good roots and merits; 9) a difference in birth in that he is born in the lineage of the Tathāgatas; 10) a difference in manifestation in that he is always able to appear in the great assemblies of Buddha's sons in order to uphold the true doctrine; and 11) a difference in results in that his results are the ten powers, the fearlessnesses, the exclusive Buddha qualities, and the arising of untold good qualities.

16. Herein two stanzas [on the four inquiries] state:

The bodhisattva must inquire into the fact that
The interdependence of name and object is incidental.
He must meditate on the duality [of their essences]
as unitary,
And as a conventional designation [of their differences].
From this he engenders reality wisdom, apart from
Objectifying the three ideas [of name, essence, and
difference].
If he sees that these do not exist,

He enters into the three absences of essence.

17. Two further stanzas on the true teaching, as given in the *Treatise on Meditating on Conscious Construction* (*Fen pieh kuan lun*), state:

In states of quiescence the bodhisattva
Understands that images exist only in his mind,
And, abandoning externalized ideas of objects,
He assuredly understands them to be only his own
thoughts.
Abiding within himself, the bodhisattva
Understands that the objective realm does not exist,
And also that the subjective realm is empty.
He then directly experiences the unobtainability of both.

18. Five verses from the *Ornament of Scriptures of the Great Vehicle* (*Mahāyānasūtrālaṃkāra*) illustrate the point:

Having nurtured the two stores of merit
And wisdom without limit,
A bodhisattva, in virtue of his certainty
In reflection on doctrine,
Is able to understand that the varied objects
Are caused by ideas.

Knowing that the varied objects are only ideas,
He abides in conscious construction-only,
Wherein objects appear.
Therefore a practitioner of meditation realizes
The Dharma realm
And is liberated both from duality and
From a nonduality [that would ignore those appearances].

If one knows that there nothing remains apart from mind,
Then he realizes also that mind does not exist either.
Seeing both to be nonexistent, the sage
Abides in the true reality realm of nonduality.

The sage, through nonimaginative wisdom
Is constantly impartial in all his actions,
And the dense thicket of
Error with its defiled support is banished and eliminated,
Just as a medicine expels a poison.

The sage, who is well-grounded in the true doctrine
Taught by the Buddha,
Places his mind at its root upon the reality realm and,
Knowing that memory is merely imagination,
Arrives at the shore of the ocean of good qualities.[20]

Chapter IV

The Distinguishing Characteristics of the Cause and Result of This Entry

1. We have now explained the entry into the distinguishing characteristics of the knowable. How then should we understand the distinguishing characteristics of the cause and result of this entry?

By means of the six perfections: giving (*dāna*), discipline (*śīla*), patience (*kṣānti*), zeal (*vīrya*), meditation (*dhyāna*), and wisdom (*prajñā*).

How are these six perfections the cause for gaining insight into conscious construction-only? How are they the result of such insight?

All bodhisattvas who abide within this true doctrine are unat- 124b
tached to their own prosperity. They are without fault against discipline. They are not worried over suffering. They are not lazy or indolent in meditation. Thus being unfettered to the causes of distraction, they constantly practice one-pointedness of mind, and examining all things in truth they gain insight into conscious construction-only.

Having already entered the realm of conscious construction-only, in virtue of these six perfections, the bodhisattvas then attain the six perfections of a purified and committed disposition. Therefore even if they do not intensify their efforts in regard to the six perfections, in [their] commitment to true discourse and in their reflections of spiritual relish, pleasure, and delight, they continually cultivate [the six perfections] without respite. Therefore they cultivate the six perfections to their final fullness.

2. In reference to this stanzas state:

Cultivating radiant qualities to perfection,
Bodhisattvas attain a subtle patience in

This great discourse [on the perfections], deep and broad,
Of their own vehicle.

Aware that there are only ideas and
Attaining a wisdom that clings not,
Their purity of commitment
Is described as a stage of purified disposition.

Abiding in the outflow of doctrine,
Bodhisattvas see all Buddhas, past and future;
Knowing that awakening is near,
Without difficulty they will attain it easily.

3. (Placed at end of this chapter under number 14.)

4. Why are there only six perfections? Because there are only six defiled obstacles that they are meant to counter, because they are the basis for all Buddha qualities, and because they are a support toward maturing all sentient beings.

The perfections of giving and discipline are meant to counter the causes that prevent embarking [upon the religious life], i.e., attachment to possessions and home. When one has embarked upon practice, the perfections of patience and zeal are meant to counter the causes of retrogression and spiritual debility, i.e., the opposition from other transmigrating sentient beings and weariness in one's efforts at bolstering virtues over a long period of time. After one has embarked upon practice and overcome this retrogressive debility, the perfections of meditation and wisdom are meant to counter the causes of loss, i.e., distraction and false wisdom.

Therefore the perfections are established to counter these six defiled obstacles. They are numbered as six because they are a basis for all the Buddha qualities. The first four perfections are causes of nondistraction, and the perfection [of meditation] is the essence of nondistraction. By relying on this state of nondistraction, one can truly understand the truth of all things [in the perfection of wisdom]—whereupon all the true qualities of a Tathāgata are generated. Therefore they are six because they are a basis for all the Buddha qualities and because they are a support toward maturing all sentient beings. The perfection of giving succors sentient beings. The perfection of discipline avoids injury to sentient beings. The perfection of patience enables those who suffer abuse from others to avoid feelings of revenge. The perfection of zeal brings forth good roots in others and eliminates bad roots. Thus benefited in this fashion, all sentient beings become docile and their distracted minds are led to concentration, and thence to liberation, for this is the significance of meditation and wisdom. Because bodhisattvas teach them through these six perfections, sentient beings mature. They are six because they support the maturation of sentient beings. These are the reasons why there are six perfections. 124c

5. What are the distinguishing characteristics of the six perfections? They are all characterized through six kinds of excellences: 1) unparalleled support—their support is the arising of the mind of supreme awakening; 2) unparalleled resources—all three levels of resources that are attributed to the perfections are fully cultivated by the bodhisattvas; 3) unparalleled tasks—the tasks of gladdening and benefiting sentient beings, for all the perfections of bodhisattvas are intended to accomplish these two tasks; 4) unparalleled skillful means, i.e., nonimaginative wisdom—all the perfections practiced by the bodhisattvas are included within their nonimaginative wisdom; 5) unparalleled orientation—all the perfections practiced by the bodhisattvas who turn toward supreme awakening are assuredly directed toward the result of universal wisdom; and 6) unparalleled purification—the two obstacles of passion and to knowledge are utterly eliminated without remainder, for all the perfections practiced by bodhisattvas progressively eradicate these two obstacles until they are obliterated.

Is all giving a perfection? Are perfections always giving? It can be that giving is not a perfection and that there is a perfection that is not giving. It is also possible for giving to be a perfection and for there to be a non-perfection that is not giving. The same four possibilities apply to the other perfections also.

6. Why are the six perfections presented in the above sequence? Because the earlier ones lead toward the arising of the later ones and because the former ones are purified by the later ones.

7. What are the nominal definitions of the six perfections? From what etymologies are they derived?

The term perfection, *"pāramitā,"* means that in surpassing and going beyond the good roots of the perfections of persons in the world, word-hearers, and solitary enlightened ones, one is enabled to reach that far shore (*pāramitā*).

125a Giving, *"dāna,"* is called *"dā"* because it destroys miserly envy and eliminates bitter poverty (*dāridrya*). It is called *"na"* because it makes (*ānayati*) one a wealthy lord, prosperous and resourceful.

Discipline, *"śīla,"* is called *"śī"* because it abates (*śītīkaroti*) depraved and evil practices. It is called *"la"* because it is conducive (*laṃbhayati*) to good practices and concentration.

Patience, *"kṣānti,"* is called *"kṣā"* because it eradicates (*kṣāyati*) anger and hatred. It is called *"ti"* because it is conducive to peace (*kṣeme tiṣṭhati*) for self and others.

Zeal, *"vīrya,"* is called *"vī"* because it eradicates (*vimocayati*) indolence and evil states. It is called *"rya"* because without failure its practice leads to (*niryati*) innumerable good states.

Meditation, *"dhyāna,"* is called *"dhyā"* because it eliminates (*vidhamati*) distractions. It is called *"na"* because it elicits (*ānayati*) a mind focused on an inner object.

Wisdom, *"prajñā,"* is called *"pra"* because it eradicates (*praṇaśati*) all false views and wisdoms. It is called *"jñā"* because it truly knows (*jānāti*) all things in their varieties.

8. What are the cultivations of these perfections? In sum there are five cultivations: 1) the cultivation of methods of exercising effort, 2) the cultivation of commitment, 3) the cultivation of reflection, 4) the cultivation of eminent wisdom in skillful means, and 5) the cultivation of benefit for others. On the first four see above. The cultivation of benefit for others means that in their spontaneous activity and non-abandonment of Tathāgata deeds, all Buddhas cultivate the perfections again and again until they reach fullness.

Now the cultivation of reflection refers to the practices comprised in the reflections of spiritual relish, pleasure, and delight, [each of which] includes six aspirations: the vast aspiration, the long-term aspiration, the joyous aspiration, the benevolent aspiration, the great resolve aspiration, and the good aspiration.

[In regard to the reflection of spiritual relish], the vast aspiration means that the bodhisattva considers the millions of eons it takes him to reach supreme awakening as a single instant, and at each instant he abandons his physical life and worships the Tathāgatas, making offerings of all the seven-jeweled world realms more numerous than the sands of the Ganges River. From his initial commitment until he enters and abides in purified awakening, that bodhisattva's aspiration toward giving is insatiable. Similarly on innumerable occasions at each instant that bodhisattva, in the burning fire that fills the trichiliocosm, assumes the four deportments in all his actions and, even though bereft of all possessions, he always keeps present and practices thoughts of discipline, patience, zeal, meditation, and wisdom—until he enters and abides in the final, purified awakening. The bodhisattva's aspiration for the other perfections is also insatiable. It is this insatiable mind for the perfections that is meant by the bodhisattva's vast aspiration.

The long-term aspiration means that from his initial commitment until he becomes awakened, the bodhisattva does not abandon this insatiable mind.

The joyous aspiration means that in his deeds of benefiting 125b
others through the practices of the six perfections, the bodhisattva always elicits unparalleled joy, such as cannot be realized by those sentient beings whom he benefits.

The benevolent aspiration means that, after benefiting sentient beings through his practice of the six perfections, the bodhisattva sees those sentient beings as more benevolent than he himself, rather than the reverse.

The great resolve aspiration means that the bodhisattva provides all sentient beings with good roots of virtue generated through his six perfections and with an unattached intent directs [his meritorious efforts] to lead them to attain their longed-for reward.

The good aspiration means that the bodhisattva makes available for the common use of sentient beings all the meritorious good roots of his practice of the six perfections, so that they all may be directed toward supreme awakening.

It is thus that the bodhisattva practices the reflection of spiritual relish embodied in these six aspirations.

The bodhisattva's reflection of spiritual pleasure embodied in the six aspects means that he takes pleasure in the meritorious good roots engendered in these six aspects by innumerable other bodhisattvas.

The bodhisattva's reflection of spiritual delight embodied in these six aspirations means that he delights in all sentient beings cultivating the six perfections with these six aspirations and that he himself vows to do the same until such practices lead to awakening.

Those who hear about the bodhisattva's practice of reflection in these six aspirations and who engender a single mind of faith will attain immeasurable and limitless accumulations of merits; and all obstacles from their evil actions will be utterly obliterated. If ordinary people, upon hearing, attain such immeasurable and limitless merit, what can we say about the exhaustive practices of a bodhisattva?

9. What are the subdivisions of these perfections? Each has three subdivisions:

Giving: the giving of doctrine, of possessions, and of fearlessness.

Discipline: that which restrains, that which assembles good qualities, and that which benefits sentient beings.

Patience: that which endures harm from others, that which accepts suffering, and that which observes things [with equanimity].

Zeal: that which incites oneself to effort, that which intensifies one's efforts, and that which lacks shrinking, diminution, or satiety.

Meditation: that which establishes pleasant residences, that which engenders supernatural powers, and that which benefits others.

Wisdom: preparatory to nonimagination, nonimagination, and that which is attained subsequent to nonimagination.

10. What is the content of these perfections? All good qualities are fundamentally present in these six perfections, since these 125c [good qualities] are the outflowing results of these perfections and since [the perfections] are conducive to all good qualities.

11. How does one know that the [vices] opposed to these perfections include all the passions? Because of their nature [as attachment], because they cause the arising of those [states of greed, anger, and delusion], and because they are the results that flow from those states.

12. What are the merits of these perfections? In their transmigratory course bodhisattvas [by means of these perfections] have mastery over positions of great wealth, high birth, an assembly of followers, success in their efforts to produce great riches, absence of sickness and pain, a lessening of desire, and intelligence in all arts and learning. At will, without losing the pleasures of their wealth, they benefit sentient beings, since this is their proper activity. The merits of the six perfections cultivated by those bodhisattvas remain unchanging until they enter and abide in final, purified awakening.

13. What is the reciprocity between the perfections? The World-honored One has spoken of all these perfections under the name of any single perfection, for his intent was to show that the cultivation of any perfection is aided by all the others.

14. Here a stanza states:

Number, character, sequence,
Names, cultivations, subdivisions, and content,
[Vices] countered, merits, and reciprocity,
Demonstrate the significance of the perfections.

Chapter V

The Distinguishing Characteristics of the Diverse Practices in Regard to Entering the Cause and Result

1. We have now explained the distinguishing characteristics of the cause and result of entry into the characteristics [of the knowable]. What then are the excellences in [practicing] the causes and [achieving] the results of this entry?

They are the ten bodhisattva stages: 1) the stage of joy (*pramuditā-bhūmi*), 2) the stage of stainlessness (*vimalā-bhūmi*), 3) the stage of bright radiance (*prabhākarī-bhūmi*), 4) the stage of blazing fire (*arciṣmatī-bhūmi*), 5) the stage difficult to conquer (*sudurjayā-bhūmi*), 6) the stage of presence (*abhimukhī-bhūmi*), 7) the far-reaching stage (*dūraṃgamā-bhūmi*), 8) the stage of imperturbability (*acalā-bhūmi*), 9) the stage of subtle wisdom (*sādhumatī-bhūmi*), and 10) the stage of the Dharma cloud (*dharmameghā-bhūmi*).

Why is their number fixed at ten? Because they counter the 126a
ten ignorances that occlude these stages, for the ten ignorances act as obstacles to the ten manifestations of the reality realm. What are the characteristics of these ten manifestations of the reality realm?

In the first stage one should understand the reality realm as omnipresent. In the second stage one should understand the reality realm as most excellent. In the third stage one should understand the reality realm as an excellent outflow. In the fourth stage one should understand the reality realm as ungraspable. In the fifth stage one should understand the reality realm as undifferentiated in its continuity. In the sixth stage one should understand the reality realm as undefiled and unpurified. In the seventh stage one should understand the reality realm as undivided by multiplicity. In the eighth stage one should understand the reality realm as without increase or decrease. In the ninth stage one should understand the reality realm as supporting the mastery of concentrations, lands, and wisdoms. In the tenth stage one should understand the reality realm as supporting mastery over actions and the methods of meditative formulas and concentrations. On this point stanzas state:

> Omnipresent and most excellent,
> Excellent outflow and ungraspable,
> Undifferentiated and neither defiled nor purified,
> Undivided by multiplicity,
> Without increase or decrease, and
> Supporting four kinds of mastery—
> Support for actions, as well as for formulas and
> concentrations.

These two stanzas from the *Analysis of the Middle and the Extremes* should be understood. Note that these ignorances are [considered to be] undefiled for adherents of the two vehicles, but defiled for bodhisattvas.

2. Why is the first stage called that of joy? Because therein one first attains the ability to benefit both self and others.

Why is the second stage called that of stainlessness? Because therein one is far removed from stains that would violate the bodhisattva discipline.

Why is the third stage called that of bright radiance? Because therein, relying on unfaltering concentrations and contemplations, one supports the light of the great doctrine.

Why is the fourth stage called that of blazing fire? Because therein the virtues favorable to awakening burn up all obstacles.

Why is the fifth stage called difficult to conquer? Because therein the two wisdoms of truth and convention stand in sharp contrast and are difficult to unify and bring together.

Why is the sixth stage called that of presence? Because therein, relying on a wisdom of the twelvefold dependent co-arising, one is able to bring to presence the perfection of wisdom.

Why is the seventh stage called far-reaching? Because therein one arrives at the final limit through energetic practices.

Why is the eighth stage called that of imperturbability? Because therein one cannot be moved by any image or mental activity.

Why is the ninth stage called that of subtle wisdom? Because therein one supports the most excellent and unoccluded wisdoms of investigation.

Why is the tenth stage called that of the Dharma cloud? Because therein an awareness of the unity of all doctrines lies silent 126b
within meditative formulas and concentrations, because one removes from view the gross obstacles, just as a cloud covers the sky, and because one brings the Dharma body to perfection.

3. How does one attain these stages? In four ways: 1) in virtue of having attained commitment, i.e., one assuredly engenders commitment at each stage; 2) in virtue of having attained practice, i.e., one has attained the ten true practices of doctrine proper to each stage; 3) in virtue of having attained penetration, i.e., when one has first penetrated to the reality realm of suchness at the first stage, he can then penetrate all stages; and 4) in virtue of attaining accomplishment, i.e., one arrives at the summit of practice through these ten stages.

4. How should one describe the practices of these stages? When all the bodhisattvas in each and every stage embark on their practices of quietude and insight, they accomplish them through five practices: 1) general practice, 2) practice without images, 3) effortless practice, 4) fervent practice, and 5) insatiable practice. All the stages have these five practices.

These five practices in all stages engender five results: 1) at each instant one can destroy the bases for all downward proclivities; 2) one transcends the confused notion of multiplicity and delights in doctrine; 3) one sees the light of the good doctrine everywhere as unlimited and undiscriminated; 4) as the pattern of imagining is converted, one attains the constant pattern of its purified aspect, and his continuity [of consciousness] fully perfects the Dharma body; and 5) one assembles the proper causes, stretching continuously forth from one high stage to the next.

5. In these ten stages one practices the ten perfections in sequence. In the first six stages one practices the six corresponding perfections, while in the later four stages, the four [further] perfections are practiced: 1) the perfection of skillful means—one gives the merits from good roots nurtured through the six perfections to all sentient beings equally so that they may be directed toward supreme awakening; 2) the perfection of vows—this perfection encompasses the variety of vows whereby one excites future causes for engendering the six perfections; 3) the perfection of powers—through the practices of thoughtful investigation, powers subdue everything that counters the perfections and brings forth the six perfections in an uninterrupted continuity; 4) the perfection of knowledge—this perfection establishes the understanding of the first six perfections and causes bodhisattvas in the great assemblies to experience delight in doctrine and to mature sentient beings.

The last four perfections are comprised within that wisdom that is attained subsequently to nonimagination.

As taught in the scriptural collections on the perfections, not all the perfections are practiced simultaneously in all stages. Indeed, these teachings [in the scriptures] explain all this in detail.

126c 6. In practicing the ten stages, when does one arrive at their fullness?

Practitioners arrive at their fullness in five gradations—some after three incalculable eons, some after seven, and some after thirty-three.

What are these five gradations? [In the case of those who will arrive after three eons,] the practitioner engaged in [the first gradation of] practicing resolve completes [this gradation] in one incalculable eon [before entry into the ten stages]. That practitioner is engaged in [the second gradation of] practicing purified aspiration [after entry into the stages], in [the third gradation of] practicing with images [from the first to the sixth stages], and in [the fourth gradation of] practicing without images [after the seventh stage], which accounts for the second incalculable eon. Thereafter, that practitioner is engaged in [the fifth gradation of] effortlessly practicing [without images] until in the tenth stage he completes the third incalculable eon.

At times it takes seven incalculable eons. Before entering the stages there are three: one eon in being undetermined, one in being determined, and one in receiving a prophecy [of awakening]. During the stages there are four eons: one based on reality and truth, one based on abandonment, one based on quiescence, and one based on wisdom.

At times it takes thirty-three. Three eons in the stage of skillful means: one of faith practice, one of zealous practice, and one of oriented practice. Then for each of the ten stages there are three eons: entry, abiding, and departure. Thus the ten stages of true practice are fulfilled over these eons.

> With good roots and vow power,
> Firmness of intent and excellence of progress,
> In three incalculable eons,
> It is said, true practice becomes perfected.

Chapter VI

The Distinguishing Characteristics of Learning Discipline

1. We have now explained the excellences in the practices of the causes of entry and its results. What then are the distinguishing features of learning discipline?

It is as taught in the chapter "On Receiving the Bodhisattva Discipline" in the *Bodhisattva Stages* (*Bodhisattvabhūmi*). In summary there are four excellences: 1) excellence in its varieties, 2) excellence in its common and specific rules, 3) excellence in its extensiveness, and 4) excellence in its profundity.

2. Its excellence in varieties is threefold: discipline that restrains, discipline that accumulates good states, and discipline that benefits sentient beings.

Herein discipline that restrains is the support of the other two. Furthermore discipline that accumulates good states is the support for engendering the Buddha qualities, while discipline that benefits sentient beings is the support for maturing sentient beings.

3. Its excellence in rules common [also to the discipline of word-hearers] means that this is a discipline whereby the bodhisattva is far removed from what is fundamentally sinful [such as murder, theft, and illicit sensual desire].

Its excellence in rules specific [to bodhisattvas] indicates a discipline whereby a bodhisattva is far removed from prohibitions about sin—thus where a word-hearer would sin, a bodhisattva 127a
remains sinless or, contrariwise, a bodhisattva can sin where a word-hearer would remain innocent. Bodhisattva discipline governs [acts of] body, speech, and mind, while a word-hearer's discipline governs only [acts of] body and speech. Therefore mental sins can occur for a bodhisattva that do not hold for a word-hearer.

In sum the benefit to sentient beings brought about by his acts of body, speech, and mind are faultless. In such deeds all bodhisattvas must put into practice the training they have received. This is how to understand the excellence of these disciplines, both common and specific.

4. Its excellence in extensiveness has four varieties: 1) the extensiveness of [the bodhisattva's] many immeasurable trainings, 2) the extensiveness whereby he embraces immeasurable merits, 3) the extensiveness whereby he embraces the aspiration toward joy and benefit for all sentient beings, and 4) the extensiveness that supports supreme awakening.

5. Its excellence in profundity means that even if a bodhisattva would in his superior wisdom and as a skillful means commit the ten [sinful] acts of murder, and so on, he would nevertheless remain unsullied and guiltless, gaining instead immeasurable merits and quickly attaining the excellent result of supreme awakening.

Furthermore the acts of body and speech brought about through transformation also pertain to the profound discipline of a bodhisattva. Through such discipline at times he assumes the role of a king, even inflicting torment on sentient beings to establish them in the code of discipline. Or he may manifest varieties of former lives, thereby bringing some to suffer distress and resentment against their suffering, while he leads others by cajoling, benefiting, and bringing them security. When they have first elicited a mind of faith, then he causes them to mature their good roots in the holy paths of the three vehicles. This is the excellence of the bodhisattva's profundity of discipline.

6. These fourfold excellences summarize the discipline upheld by the bodhisattva. In virtue of these the superiority of his discipline is incalculable, as the Buddha taught in the *Extensive Scripture on the Call to Discipline* (*P'i na yeh ch'ü sha p'i fo lüeh ching*).

Chapter VII

The Distinguishing Characteristics of Thought Training

1. We have explained above the excellence of training in discipline. What then is the excellence of thinking? In sum it is sixfold: 1) its object, 2) its varieties, 3) its countering force, 4) its aptitude, 5) its evocations, and 6) its deeds.

2. Its object: [this thinking] focuses on the doctrine of the Great Vehicle.

3. Its varieties: it encompasses sundry states of concentration, such as the Great Vehicle light concentration, the merit-accumulation royal concentration, the illustrious protector concentration, and the heroic march concentration.

4. Its countering force: focusing on the pervasive meaning of all things, this wisdom uproots all the debilitating obstacles in the foundational consciousness, just as one wedge dislodges another wedge. 127b

5. Its aptitude: maintaining concentrated joy in this present world, one can at will be born into eminent stations.

6. Its evocations: it can elicit unhindered supernatural faculties in all world realms.

7. Its deeds: it engenders and is endowed with the great supernatural powers, to make [worlds] tremble, to blaze up, to pervade [with light], to bring about manifestations, to transform things, to go and to come, to bring near that which is far, to render minute that which is large and vice versa, to incorporate all material forms [in the universe] into one's own body, to take on the same form [as those to be saved] in entering the great assemblies, to appear and disappear, to suppress and block the supernatural powers of others through the eight masteries, whether to bestow on others abilities, memory, and happiness or to emit light on them.

8. It can engender all deeds, difficult and true, for it embraces the ten true deeds that are difficult to practice: 1) the difficult practice of one's own personal acceptance, in taking on the good vows for awakening; 2) the difficult practice of not faltering, for the many sufferings of transmigration do not cause one to turn back; 3) the difficult practice of not turning one's back, despite the fact that the evil done by sentient beings confronts one on all sides; 4) the difficult practice of being visible, for one is present to resentful sentient beings in bringing benefit to them; 5) the difficult practice of being undefiled, for bodhisattvas born into the world are not defiled by worldly conditions; 6) the difficult practice of being committed, for in practicing the unplumbable Great Vehicle one is committed to its broad and deep meaning; 7) the difficult practice of clearly understanding, for one clearly understands the non-self of both persons and things; 8) the difficult practice of comprehending, for one truly discerns the scriptures of implicit meaning of all Tathāgatas; 9) the difficult practice of not abandoning nor being defiled, for while not rejecting transmigration one is not defiled by it; and 10) the difficult practice of exerting effort in difficult tasks, for all Buddha Tathāgatas, liberated from all obstacles, spontaneously bring benefit to all sentient beings and, until the final limit of transmigration is over, desire to cultivate such efforts.

9. In regard to the difficult practice of comprehension [as treated above in number eight], how is one to understand the implicit meaning of the scriptures preached by all the Buddha Tathāgatas?

As the scriptures teach, a bodhisattva must investigate according to truth [and not according to literal sense].

How is it that [a scripture reports that] a bodhisattva neither loses anything nor gives to anyone? In that a bodhisattva has well practiced giving everywhere in an unlimited and incalculable fashion, his practice of giving arises in continuity [even though he does not at any particular moment give anything to anyone].

How is it that [a scripture reports that] a bodhisattva takes pleasure in giving? In that he does not take pleasure in any gift.

How is it that [a scripture reports that] a bodhisattva believes in giving? In that he does not place his faith in any Buddha Tathāgata.

How is it that [a scripture reports that] a bodhisattva initiates giving? In that in his giving he does not lay plans for himself.

How is it that [a scripture reports that] a bodhisattva constantly delights in giving? In that he has no moment of giving.

How is it that [a scripture reports that] a bodhisattva is capable of great giving? In that he has no rigidity in his giving. 127c

How is it that [a scripture reports that] a bodhisattva is pure in his giving? In that he engenders avarice.

How is it that [a scripture reports that] a bodhisattva is perfected in giving? In that he does not perfect any final point.

How is it that [a scripture reports that] a bodhisattva masters giving? In that he attains no mastery over his giving.

How is it that [a scripture reports that] a bodhisattva is inexhaustible in giving? In that he does not reach inexhaustibility.

One should understand the other perfections of discipline, patience, zeal, meditation, and wisdom according to the principle employed in these scriptural passages on giving.

10. Further scriptural passages say: how is it that a bodhisattva kills living beings? In that he cuts off the [transmigratory] continuity of living beings.

How is it that a bodhisattva takes what is not given to him by others? In that he takes sentient beings not given to him by others.

How is it that a bodhisattva acts perversely and lewdly? In that he elicits thoughts about the perversity of the sensual desire [of sentient beings].

How is it that a bodhisattva speaks falsehood? In that he identifies what is false as false.

How is it that a bodhisattva tells lies? In that he abides in the utmost emptiness [from which all worlds are lies].

How is it that a bodhisattva utters harsh words? In that he reaches the far shore of knowledge.

How is it that a bodhisattva utters inappropriate speech? In that he divides the doctrine and interprets it according to its genre.

How is it that a bodhisattva becomes covetous? In that he repeatedly himself attains all the unexcelled concentrations.

How is it that a bodhisattva becomes mean? In that he attacks all the passions in his own mind and the minds of others.

How is it that a bodhisattva engenders false views? In that he truly examines falsity everywhere and at all times.

11. Other scriptures discourse on the profundity of the Buddha qualities. What are these profundities? In this treatise we shall analyze them extensively [in Chapter X].

Eternity is the nature of all Buddha qualities, because the Dharma body is eternal.

Abandonment is the nature of all Buddha qualities, because all obstacles are completely severed.

Arising is the nature of all Buddha qualities, because transformation bodies constantly arise.

Attainment is the nature of all Buddha qualities, because one attains the parallel counteragent to the eighty-four thousand passionate actions of sentient beings.

Desire is the nature of all Buddha qualities, because one fulfills his identity by encompassing desire-filled sentient beings. [Similarly,] hatred, delusion, and worldliness are the nature of all Buddha qualities.

Nondefilement is the nature of all Buddha qualities, because, having fully realized suchness, no obstacle can defile [him].

Undefileability is the nature of all Buddha qualities, because, although Buddhas appear in the world, they cannot become defiled by worldly things.

These are the reasons for the profundity of the Buddha attributes.

12. It is in order to cultivate the perfections, to mature sen-
128a tient beings, to purify Buddha lands, and to generate all the Buddha attributes that the actions of the concentrations of a bodhisattva are differentiated.

Chapter VIII

The Distinguishing Characteristics of Learning Wisdom

1. We have now explained the excellence of training in thinking. What then is the excellence in wisdom training? The excellence of wisdom training consists in the superiority of nonimaginative wisdom in 1) its essence, 2) its support, 3) its cause, 4) its object, 5) its modality, 6) its establishment, 7) its solution of difficulties, 8) its maintenance, 9) its aids, 10) its reward, 11) its outflow, 12) its issue, 13) its term in practicing goodness, 14) its undifferentiated exercise of the good attributes of preparatory, nonimaginative, and subsequently attained wisdoms, 15) examples of nonimaginative and subsequently attained wisdoms, 16) its august and spontaneous activity, and 17) its profundity.

2. The essence of nonimaginative wisdom is liberation from five states: 1) from unreflectiveness, 2) from the absence of insight, 3) from a concentrated quietude that eliminates thinking and perceiving, 4) from being engrossed in material things, and 5) from differentiating imagination in regard to the meaning of reality. Nonimaginative wisdom, identified as the wisdom that is liberated from these five states, is described in the [following] verses:

[Essence:]

For all bodhisattvas, the essence [of nonimaginative wisdom]
Is liberation from the five states,
For nonimaginative wisdom is nonimaginative
In regard to reality.

3. [Support:]

For all bodhisattvas the support is

Neither thinking nor the absence of thinking,
For nonimaginative wisdom is not a not-thinking
But is something that rapidly [issues from thinking].

4. [Cause:]

For all bodhisattvas the cause is
The permeation of hearing [scriptural] discourse,
For nonimaginative wisdom is
True and correct reflection.

5. [Object:]

For all bodhisattvas the object is
Ineffable reality,
For nonimaginative wisdom [realizes]
The true suchness of the non-essence of both [self and things].

6. [Modality:]

For all bodhisattvas its modality is
Focused on true suchness,
For nonimaginative wisdom is
Imageless and undifferentiated.

7. [Establishment:]

Only meanings that are basically connected
Are discriminated, no others.
Since words form a continuum,
Its meaning is established by conjunction.

[Solution of difficulties:]

Apart from words and language
Wisdom does not occur in regard to knowables.
[But] since the two [words and knowables] are not the same,
Everything is inexpressible.

8. [Maintenance:]

The firm basis for all bodhisattvas is 128b
Nonimaginative wisdom,
For it supports practices subsequently attained
In their development to final perfection.

9. [Aids:]

For all bodhisattvas the aids
Are the two paths,
For nonimaginative wisdom is characterized
By the mental states of the [first] five perfections.

10. [Reward:]

For all bodhisattvas the reward occurs in
The two assemblies [of the transformation and
    enjoyment bodies],
For nonimaginative wisdom [arises] in virtue of
Preparatory effort and attainment [respectively].

11. [Outflow:]

For all bodhisattvas the outflow occurs
In one life after another,
For nonimaginative wisdom
Develops and progresses.

12. [Issue:]

For all bodhisattvas the issue
Is yoked to attainment and perfection,
For nonimaginative wisdom
Is known in the ten stages.

13. [Term:]

For all bodhisattvas, the term
Is the attainment of the purified three bodies,

For nonimaginative wisdom
Reaches the most excellent mastery.

14. [Preparatory wisdom:]

This nonimaginative wisdom is
Like space, undefiled
By sundry and grievous evil acts,
Simply because of its commitment.

[Nonimaginative wisdom:]

Pure like space,
This nonimaginative wisdom
Is liberated from all obstacles,
Because it has reached perfection.

[Subsequently attained wisdom:]

Undefiled like space,
This nonimaginative wisdom,
Even though it appears in the world,
Is not defiled by worldly things.

15. [Examples of these three wisdoms:]

These three wisdoms are
Like a mute who tries to perceive objects,
Like a mute who does perceive objects, and
Like a non-mute who does perceive objects.

These three wisdoms are
Like a fool who tries to perceive objects,
Like a fool who does perceive objects, and
Like a non-fool who does perceive objects.

These three wisdoms are
Like the five senses that try to perceive objects,
Like the five senses that do perceive objects, and

Like that which is not the five senses [i.e., the thinking
consciousness] that does perceive objects.

These three wisdoms are respectively
Like one of no learning who seeks to understand [a doctrine],
Like one who is well-read who does understand
[the text of] a doctrine, and
Like one who understands and perceives the meaning
of a doctrine.

16.

Nonimaginative wisdom is
Like a person who has his eyes closed.
Subsequently attained wisdom is
Like a person who has his eyes opened.

Nonimagination is like space,
Without defilement, obstruction, differentiation, or limit.
Subsequently attained wisdom is 128c
Like the appearance of forms in that space.

17. [Spontaneity:]

Just as *maṇi*-jewels or heavenly drums
Accomplish their deeds without reflection,
Just so, without discrimination,
The various Buddha deeds are accomplished.

18. [Profundity:]

This wisdom called nonimaginative
Is not differentiated from its object,
Either as this or not as this [object],
Either as not wisdom or as not not wisdom.

The Buddha has taught that all things
Are originally not imagined,
Because that which is imagined does not exist.

In light of their nonexistence, there is nonimaginative
[wisdom].

19. Herein nonimaginative wisdom is of three varieties: 1) preparatory nonimaginative wisdom, 2) nonimaginative wisdom, and 3) wisdom attained subsequent to nonimagination.

The preparatory nonimaginative wisdom has also three varieties inasmuch as it arises 1) from causes, 2) from evocation, and 3) from the force of repeated cultivation.

Nonimaginative wisdom has three varieties inasmuch as it is differentiated as 1) the completion of knowing, 2) inerrancy, and 3) nonfabrication.

Wisdom attained subsequent to nonimaginative wisdom has five varieties inasmuch as its manifestations are differentiated as 1) penetration, 2) memory, 3) presentation, 4) synthesis, and 5) magical creations.

20. The following stanzas treat nonimaginative wisdom:

Hungry ghosts, animals, humans,
All gods—each have their own
Different ideas about a single object,
Concluding that the object [they conceptualize] is valid.

As, in regard to the past and the future,
And to dreams and double images,
Knowledge objectifies things without any existent object,
So objects are posited, even though they do not occur.

If external things became objects of understanding,
There would be no nonimaginative wisdom.
If this [wisdom] did not exist,
Then the attainment of Buddhahood would also be
impossible.

Bodhisattvas who have attained mastery
Because of the power of their commitment
Create lands at will,
As do those in concentration.

Those perfected in investigation,
Those with wisdom and concentration [understand that]
All things appear as objects
Within their own minds.

When nonimaginative wisdom is cultivated,
No object appears.
Know then that no external object exists,
And thus there is no conscious construction either.

21. Nonimaginative wisdom and the perfection of wisdom are synonymous. As a scripture teaches, "When a bodhisattva dwells in the perfection of wisdom through the cultivation of non-abiding, he is able to cultivate the other perfections to their fullness." Why is it that by cultivating non-abiding he can cultivate these 129a
other perfections to their fullness? Because he is liberated from five kinds of abiding: 1) from abiding in a clinging to the self of the heretics, 2) from abiding in the imagination of bodhisattvas who have not yet gained insight into reality, 3) from abiding in the two extreme views on transmigration and cessation, 4) from abiding in being content merely with the elimination of obstacles, and 5) from abiding in cessation without remainder in disregard of benefit to sentient beings.

22. How then does the wisdom of word-hearers differ from that of bodhisattvas?

It differs because of nonimaginative wisdom, since [bodhisattvas] do not imagine things, such as the aggregates, and so on. It differs in not being incomplete, since [bodhisattvas] penetrate the two emptinesses [of self and things], enter into an understanding of all the knowables, and maintain actions to benefit all sentient beings. It differs in not abiding [in cessation], since [bodhisattvas] abide in a non-abiding cessation. It differs in duration, since [bodhisattvas] do not fall away and cut themselves off for good in cessation without remainder. It differs in supremacy, because in truth no other vehicle is above this vehicle. On this point a stanza states:

Because of the five superiorities in wisdom [of bodhisattvas] and
On account of their compassion and cultivation of merit,
In riches both mundane and transcendent,
We say they are not far from perfection.

23. If there really are such bodhisattvas who are encountered in the world, who, having accumulated merit through their trainings in discipline, concentration, and wisdom (i.e., the three trainings), have reached the ten masteries and attained unequaled and preeminent capabilities to benefit others, then why do we still see sentient beings encountering severe penury and suffering in the world?

This is because bodhisattvas see that, if they were to bestow riches, the actions of sentient beings in their consequent stage of wealth would constitute obstacles that would result in suffering and that this would hinder the good that they [otherwise] might engender. It is because bodhisattvas see that if they lack riches, they will be able to realize detestation of evil transmigration. It is because bodhisattvas see that if they were to bestow riches on them, then they would nurture the causes for all manner of evil states. It is because bodhisattvas see that if they were to bestow riches on them, this would be cause for them to oppress an untold number of other sentient beings.[21]

These are the reasons why, although bodhisattvas are not lacking in such capabilities, yet [poor and suffering] sentient beings are seen in the world.

On this point a stanza states:

Seeing the obstacle of their actions, the good hindered,
The manifestation of detestation, and increase of evil,
And the injury to other sentient beings,
Bodhisattvas are not moved toward giving [them riches].

Chapter IX

The Distinguishing Characteristics of Quiescent Abandonment as a Result of the Trainings

1.We have now treated the excellence of wisdom training. How then should we understand the excellence of quiescent abandonment?

The destruction of defilement by bodhisattvas is their non-abiding cessation. What are its characteristics? It is characterized by a twofold conversion of support whereby they definitively abandon defilement but not transmigration.

Herein transmigration refers to the defiled aspect of the other-dependent pattern. Cessation refers to the purified aspect of the other-dependent pattern. The basic support refers to both these 129b
aspects of the purified and defiled other-dependent pattern. The conversion of support means that, when its counteragent arises, the other-dependent pattern forever alters its basic nature as the defiled aspect and forever realizes its purified aspect.

2. This conversion of support has six varieties: 1) conversion that increases power and decreases abilities, because the power of the permeations of hearing at the stage of commitment [increases] while the shameful actions of the passions gradually weaken or entirely cease to function; 2) conversion of penetration—for all bodhisattvas who have ascended to the stages, manifestations of both reality and illusion are possible. This conversion occurs from the first to the sixteenth stages; 3) conversion of practice—no images appear in the supporting [consciousness] of those not yet freed from the obstacle [to the knowable], but reality does appear. This conversion occurs from the seventh to the

tenth stages; 4) conversion to the fullness of result—no images appear in the supporting [consciousness] of those who have been freed from the obstacle [to the knowable], but purified suchness appears until one attains mastery over all images; 5) inferior conversion—the realization by word-hearers of the non-self of persons, which completely turns away from transmigration and constitutes an eternal rejection of transmigration; 6) extensive conversion—the realization by bodhisattvas of the non-self of things, wherein by understanding the merits of quietude and insight, they both abandon and do not abandon [transmigration].

What fault would there be for a bodhisattva to remain in an inferior conversion? He would fail to perceive what is of benefit to sentient beings, be far distant from all bodhisattva states, and attain a liberation identical to that of the adherents of the lesser vehicles.

What merit is there in a bodhisattva maintaining an extensive conversion? Because in transmigratory conditions he converts his own support, he attains mastery in all destinies, and he manifests his bodies both in valued positions in the world and in the three vehicles. His skillful capability in various ways of teaching and converting establishes others in the true teaching. This is the merit of an extensive conversion.

3. On this point stanzas state:

For common worldlings, reality covered over
Appears to them as illusion.
For bodhisattvas, having abandoned everything,
Reality appears.

The non-appearance of illusion and
The appearance of reality are
The bodhisattva's conversion of support,
Liberation, [functioning] at will.

If wisdom engenders [insight into] the equality
Between transmigration and cessation,

Then transmigration is precisely cessation
And they are not two separate things.

Therefore in regard to transmigration
Do not abandon or refuse to abandon.
Likewise in regard to cessation
Have no attainment and no lack of attainment.

Chapter X

The Distinguishing Characteristics of the Excellence of Wisdom

1. Having explained [in the last chapter] the excellence of quiescent abandonment, we now treat the excellence of wisdom. The excellence of wisdom is to be understood as the three bodies of the Buddha, which are the essence body, the enjoyment body, and the transformation body. Among these, the essence body is the Dharma body of Tathāgatas, because it is the support for mastering all things. The enjoyment body is the body that is manifested in the various Buddha lands and assemblies of great persons. It is supported upon the Dharma body in that its cause is the complete purification of the Buddha lands and the experience of delight in the doctrine of the Great Vehicle. The transformation body is also supported upon the Dharma body because it manifests itself [in many perceptible manners], such as residing in and descending from the Tuṣita [Heaven], being born [in Kapilavastu], undertaking learning, indulging in desire for the material world, leaving home, going to the heretics' place, practicing asceticism, attaining perfect awakening, turning the wheel of the Dharma, and entering into final cessation. 129c

2. How is the Dharma body of Buddhas to be characterized? In brief, it is characterized in five manners. On this point a summary stanza states:

> Characteristic, realization and attainment, mastery, support, constitution, distinction, good qualities, profundity, recollection, and activity. These [are the themes that] clarify the Buddha bodies.

3. The Dharma body is characterized as the conversion of support because, when the [other-]dependent pattern in its defiled aspect with all its obstacles has been eliminated, one is liberated from all those obstacles and is converted into the dependent pattern in its pure aspect with mastery over all things.

It is characterized as being composed of radiant qualities because through the completion of the six perfections, one obtains the excellent capabilities of the ten masteries. Among these [ten masteries], the mastery over the duration of life, the mastery over mind, and the mastery over necessities are [obtained] through the fullness of the perfection of giving. The mastery over act and the mastery over birth are [obtained] through the fullness of the perfection of discipline. The mastery over commitment is [obtained] through the fullness of the perfection of patience. The mastery over vow is [obtained] through the fullness of the perfection of zeal. The mastery over miraculous powers, which include the five supernatural faculties, is [obtained] through the fullness of the perfection of meditation. The mastery over understanding and the mastery over doctrine are [obtained] through the fullness of the perfection of wisdom.

The Dharma body is characterized by nonduality because, being characterized by the nonduality of existence and nonexistence, all things are nonexistent and their characteristic of emptiness is not nonexistent. It is also characterized by nonduality of the conditioned and the unconditioned, because it is not engendered by acts and passions but is powerful in manifesting itself in conditioned images. It is also characterized by the nonduality of unity and differentiation, because [in the Dharma body] the support of all Buddhas is not different [the one from the other] and yet innumerable individual [bodhisattvas] attain perfect awakening. On
130a this point there are stanzas:

> Because there is no clinging to self, there is no differentiation in the support [of all Buddhas]. But since many individuals are enlightened in consequence of their former [states

> as bodhisattvas], their designated names are said not to be a unity.
>
> Because of the division of [their] lineages, of [their] usefulness, of [their] totality, of [their] beginninglessness, they are not a unity. Because of the absence of differentiation in [their] support, which is suchness, there is no multiplicity.

The Dharma body is characterized by eternity, because [it has] the purity of suchness as its characteristic, because it is under the impulse of former vows [which are never abandoned], and because its activity and action are unending.

The Dharma body is characterized by inconceivability, because the purity of suchness is to be known by a personal realization, because it cannot be compared to anything, and because it is beyond the scope of intelligent knowing.

4. How then is this Dharma body realized and attained? It is initially attained through contact by the nonimaginative and subsequently attained wisdoms, which have as their object the unified doctrine of the Great Vehicle. [These wisdoms] are accomplished, matured, and cultivated in the five aspects [of practice explained in Chapter V] and have well accumulated the equipment in all the stages [leading to Buddhahood]. [It is attained] by the diamond-like concentration, since [that concentration] destroys the subtle obstacles that are difficult to destroy. Having been separated from all obstacles immediately after that concentration, [the Dharma body] is thus acquired through the conversion of support.

5. What are the masteries whereby the Dharma body obtains mastery? In sum it obtains [such power] by five kinds: 1) mastery in manifesting Buddha lands, in his own bodies, in major and minor marks, in infinite sound, and in invisible head markings, [obtained] because the material aggregate has been converted; 2) mastery over pleasant abodes, which are irreproachable, immeasurable, and vast, [obtained] because the aggregate of sensation has been converted; 3) mastery in true teaching through all the collections of words, phrases, and sentences, [obtained] because the aggregate

of conceptualization, which is the support for the discrimination of apprehended images, has been converted; 4) mastery in transformations, in bringing about changes, in bringing together assemblies, and in bringing together radiantly pure states, [obtained] because the aggregate of volitional predisposition has been converted; and 5) mastery in [the four] wisdoms of clear manifestation, equality, returning insight, and duty fulfillment, [obtained] because the aggregate of consciousness has been converted.

6. What kinds of conditions are supported by the Dharma body? In short there are three [conditions] so supported.

The Dharma body is the support of the diverse residences of Buddha Tathāgatas, [as expressed in] the following stanzas:

> All Buddha Tathāgatas, because they have realized and attained their own realm, acquire a fivefold joy, but adherents of the two vehicles lack such a joy because they have not realized it. Therefore one who desires such joy should realize the realm of the Buddha.

> Because they are capable of establishing immeasurable deeds and because, delighting in the beauty of doctrine, their desire comes to fulfillment, Buddhas, who attain the highest, irreproachable joy, gain constant insight into the four immeasurable activities.

The Dharma body is the support for the diverse bodies of enjoyment, because [the enjoyment body] brings the good roots of bodhisattvas to maturity.

130b It is the support of the diverse bodies of transformation, because [the transformation body] generally brings word-hearers and solitary enlightened ones to maturity.

7. How many Buddha factors comprise the Dharma body? In short it is comprised by six kinds of Buddha factors: 1) the Buddha factor of purification, because the Dharma body is attained upon conversion of the container consciousness; 2) the factor of maturation, because an excellent wisdom of maturation is attained upon

the conversion of the sense organs; 3) the factor of dwelling, because a dwelling of immeasurable wisdom is attained upon the conversion of the dwellings in hedonistic behavior; 4) the factor of mastery, because supremacy in the wisdom of the six supernatural knowledges unimpeded in all the world realms is attained upon the conversion of gainful endeavors; 5) the factor of verbal expression, because supremacy in the wisdom of true teaching to satisfy the minds of all sentient beings is attained upon the conversion of verbal expressions of things seen, heard, perceived, and known; and 6) the factor of alleviation, because a wisdom that alleviates all the misfortunes and mistakes of all sentient beings is gained upon the conversion to the aspiration to alleviate all misfortune and mistakes.

The Dharma body of all Buddha Tathāgatas is to be understood as consisting of these six kinds of Buddha factors.

8. Should the Dharma body of Buddhas be expressed as differentiated or as not differentiated? It is not differentiated, because their support, their aspiration, and their deeds are not differentiated. But it is also differentiated, because innumerable [bodhisattvas] do attain perfect awakening.

Just as with the Dharma body, so the enjoyment body is also not differentiated, because its support and activity are not differentiated. However, since they are able to support differentiation, it is not the case that they are [simply] undifferentiated, for innumerable consciousnesses [of bodhisattvas] are converted [to awakening]. The transformation body is to be understood in a parallel manner.

9. With how many virtues is the Dharma body endowed? The Dharma body is endowed with the perfectly purified four immeasurable activities, the eight liberations, the eight governing spheres, the ten entire spheres, noncontentious concentration, vow wisdom, the four unimpeded understandings, the six supernatural knowledges, the thirty-two major marks of a great person, the eighty minor marks, the four purifications of all aspects, the ten powers, the four fearlessnesses, the four things that need not be guarded against, the three focuses of mindfulness, the entire destruction

of the propensities, nonforgetfulness, great compassion, the eighteen exclusive qualities of a Buddha, and the excellent wisdom of all excellent aspects.

10. Here are stanzas [on these qualities]:

[On the four immeasurable activities:]

O you who have great compassion on sentient beings, you who have the aspiration to separate [them] from bondage, you who have the aspiration not to separate [from sentient beings], you who have the aspiration for happiness and welfare—homage to you!

11. [On the liberations, the governing spheres, and the entire spheres:]

O you who are liberated from all obstacles, the sage who overcomes the entire world, you whose wisdom is universally replete, you whose mind is liberated—homage to you!

12. [On noncontentious concentration:]

O you who destroy all the passions of all sentient beings with-
130c out remainder, who crush the defilement of the passions, who
always take pity on the passionate—homage to you!

13. [On vow wisdom:]

O you who are spontaneous, unattached, unimpeded, continually quiescent, you who answer all the questions of sentient beings—homage to you!

14. [On unimpeded understandings:]

O you who are unimpeded in teaching with regard to the support and that which supports and the language and wisdom needed, you, the teacher—homage to you!

15. [On the supernatural knowledges:]

O you who, having approached [sentient beings] through their words, know their conduct in regard to their coming, going, and deliverance, you who well instruct sentient beings—homage to you!

16. [On major and minor marks:]

After having seen you, all sentient beings revere you as a noble person. O you who, upon being seen by others, inspire a purified mind—homage to you!

17. [On purifications in all aspects:]

O you who have attained mastery over concentrations and wisdoms in regard to taking up, maintaining, and forsaking [the body], and in regard to transformations and changes [in things], World-honored One—homage to you!

18. [On the powers:]

O you who shatter the demons who impede sentient beings about the means, the refuge, the purification, and the deliverance to the Great Vehicle—homage to you!

19. [On fearlessnesses:]

O you who teach understanding, abandonment, deliverance, and [the nature] of the obstacles encountered, for the benefit of both self and others, overcoming any perverse [view]—homage to you!

[On the things that need not be guarded against:]

O you who are unfettered, irreproachable, undefiled, and non-abiding, unmoved by things and unfabricating—homage to you!

20. [On mindfulness:]

O you whose speech is awesome in the assemblies, who are free from the two defilements, who have nothing to be guarded against, who forget nothing, who gather together communities—homage to you!

21. [On nonforgetfulness:]

O you who, in carrying out the interests of all sentient beings, do not waste time, whose work is never without fruit, who are never confused—homage to you!

22. [On the destruction of propensities:]

O you whose activity is perfected wisdom everywhere, whether setting out or at rest, who know all times and understand the essence of reality—homage to you!

23. [On great compassion:]

O you who continually[22] behold sentient beings in the entire world day and night, who are endowed with great compassion, who have the aspiration to benefit—homage to you!

24. [On the exclusive Buddha qualities:]

O you who are unequaled by those in the two vehicles in performance, attainments, wisdoms, and deeds—homage to you!

25. [On the excellent wisdom of all aspects:]

O you who have realized the great awakening of all aspects by the three bodies, who cut off any doubts of others—homage to you!

26.

131a O you who have no attachment, no fault, no turbidity, no stagnation, no vacillation in regard to anything, and no [conceptual] fabrication—homage to you!

27. Furthermore the Dharma body of all Buddhas is always endowed not only with these virtues but also with the qualities of essence, cause, result, activity, associated qualities, and function. Therefore the qualities of all Buddhas are to be understood as supreme. On this point stanzas state:

You have accomplished suchness, you have been delivered through cultivating all the stages, you have attained preeminence among [all] others, you are the liberator of all sentient beings.

You are associated with inexhaustible and unequaled qualities, you are seen in the world and in the three assemblies, and yet you are invisible in every way to gods and humans!

28. The Dharma body of the Tathāgatas is profound, supremely profound. How should that profundity be examined? Stanzas [on these profundities follow]:

The unborn Buddha is born, abides in non-abiding, does everything spontaneously, and eats the fourth food.

[Buddhas] are undifferentiated and immeasurable; their one activity is beyond calculation; endowed with the three bodies, their action, both continual and interrupted, is supreme.

There is nothing that can be awakened, but it is not the case that there is no perfectly awakened one at all. At every moment [Buddhas] are immeasurable and are manifested through the nonexistence of existence.

[The Buddha] is neither attached nor detached and is delivered by desire itself. After having known desire and nondesire, he has entered into the reality of desire.

The Buddha has gone beyond the five aggregates, and yet he dwells in the five aggregates. He is neither identical with nor separated from the aggregates, for he has entered a cessation that does not abandon the aggregates.

All the actions of Buddhas completely interpenetrate just like water in the ocean. They have no intention of benefiting others, [such as] thinking "I have done, am doing, or will do [such a deed for others]."

The World-honored One is not seen because of the faults of sentient beings, just as the moon [is not seen reflected] in a broken basin, [but] like the sun he fills all worlds with the light of the Dharma.

At times, like a fire, [Buddhas] manifest perfect illumination, and at times, like a fire, they are extinguished, for these two in fact do not exist, but [the Dharma body] of all Buddhas abides forever.

131b The Tathāgata abides in the supremely abiding self, in unholy conditions, in human and evil [destinies], and in unchaste conditions.

Although they move about everywhere, they do not move about at all. They do appear in all states of birth, and yet they are beyond the sphere of the six senses.

The passions [of Buddhas] have been destroyed and suppressed, just like a poison counteracted by a magical spell. They have exhausted passion through passion and have attained universal wisdom.

For those who practice the great means, passions become factors of awakening, and transmigration is identified with cessation. Therefore awakening is inconceivable.

The significance [of these stanzas] should be understood as applying to the twelve kinds of profundities. [The first treats] the profundity of birth, non-abiding, actions, and sustenance. [The second treats] the profundity of place, number, and activity. [The third treats] the profundity of perfect awakening. [The fourth treats] the profundity of detachment. [The fifth treats] the profundity of the abandonment of aggregates. [The sixth treats] the profundity of maturing [sentient beings]. [The seventh treats] the profundity of manifesting. [The eighth treats] the profundity of manifesting awakening and cessation. [The ninth treats] the profundity of dwelling. [The tenth treats] the profundity of manifesting bodies.

[The eleventh treats] the profundity of the abandonment of passion. [And the twelfth treats] the profundity of inconceivability.

29. When bodhisattvas focus on the Dharma body and recollect Buddhas, how many recollections do they employ? In sum, in relying on the Dharma body they cultivate the recollection of Buddhas in seven ways. 1) They cultivate the recollection of Buddhas by considering: "All the Buddhas have unequaled mastery over all things," for they have acquired the six unimpeded and unbounded supernatural knowledges over all world realms. Here is a stanza [on this]:

> Buddhas do not have entire mastery over the realm of all those sentient beings who are obstructed, without potential, or yoked to the twofold inevitability.

2) [They cultivate the recollection of Buddhas] by considering: "The body of the Tathāgata is eternal," because, with suchness uninterrupted, they are liberated from impurities. 3) [They cultivate the recollection of Buddhas] by considering: "The Tathāgatas are supremely irreproachable," because they are forever free from all obstacles: of passion and to knowledge. 4) [They cultivate the recollection of Buddhas] by considering: "The deeds of Tathāgatas are done spontaneously," because all of their true actions, which arise spontaneously, are never abandoned. 5) [They cultivate the recollection of Buddhas] by considering: "The Tathāgatas abide in great richness and enjoyment," because all the wondrous purity of all Buddha lands is their richness and enjoyment. 6) [They cultivate the recollection of Buddhas] by considering: "The Tathāgatas are never soiled nor attached," because they are not soiled by any worldly thing, even though they depart from and appear in the world, just as dust cannot soil the sky. 7) [They cultivate the recollection of Buddhas] by considering: "The Tathāgatas are of great use in the world," because, by manifesting supreme awakening and final cessation, they mature those sentient beings who are not completely mature and liberate those who are completely mature. Here are stanzas [on these recollections]:

[Buddhas] are perfected in relying on the mind of the Tathāgata and are perfected in good qualities, in eternity, in irre-
131c proachability, in spontaneity, and in granting great joy in doctrine to sentient beings.

In all their actions they are unimpeded and equally benefit many men. Wise men should base themselves upon such recollections of all Buddhas universally.

30. How is the purity of the pure land of all Buddha Tathāgatas to be understood? In the manner in which it is described in the preface of the *One Hundred Thousand-Stanza Scripture* (*Pai ch'ien ching*) of the bodhisattva-*piṭaka,* [which recounts that] the World-honored Buddha dwells in a great palace.

The Buddha dwells in a great palace, which is ornamented with the seven gems and emits a great light completely filling immeasurable world realms. The configuration of its immeasurable and wondrous distribution of ornaments constitutes a vast area. Its boundaries cannot be crossed or measured. Its domain transcends the activity and domain of the triple world. It arises from good states beyond world-transcendence. It is characterized by a masterfully engendered and well purified conscious construction. It is the abode of Tathāgatas. It is the refuge of bodhisattvas. It is the immeasurable promenade of gods, *nāga*s, *yakṣa*s, *asura*s, *garuḍa*s, *kiṃnara*s, *mahoraga*s, humans, and those who are not human. It is sustained by great enjoyment and delight in the taste of doctrine. It functions in bringing about all benefit for all sentient beings. It is removed from the torment of all the passions. Inimical forces are not active there. Surpassing all arrays, it is an abode arrayed by the Tathāgata. Its deliverance is by great memory, understanding, and practice. Its vehicles are great tranquility and insight. Its entrances are the great liberation gates of emptiness, imagelessness, and desirelessness. It rests upon the great lotus king, ornamented with innumerable collections of good qualities.

The Tathāgata dwells in this great palace. Thus the pure land is completely purified in color, configuration, extent, domain, cause, result, lords, confreres, servants, sustenance, action, beneficence, fearlessness, abode, path, vehicles, entrance gates, and foundation. In these above descriptions its complete purity is manifested. The enjoyment of the perfectly purified Buddha land is completely pure, completely pleasurable, completely irreproachable, completely masterful.

31. It should be understood that the Dharma realm of Buddhas 132a
is endowed with five functions at all times: 1) it has the function of rescuing beings from misery, since merely by a glance such diseases as blindness, deafness, and idiocy can be expelled; 2) it has the function of rescuing from evil destinies, since it draws [beings] out of evil destinies and establishes them in good destinies; 3) it has the function of rescuing from unfit methods, since it suppresses the unfit methods practiced by all the heretics and establishes them in the true doctrine of the Buddha; 4) it has the function of rescuing from belief in individuality, since it can manifest a holy path and instruct in a method to cross over the triple world; and 5) it has the function of rescuing from [other] vehicles, since it introduces bodhisattvas inclined toward the practice of other vehicles and word-hearers to the practice of the Great Vehicle.

It should be understood that these five actions are the same for all Buddha Tathāgatas. Here is a stanza on this [equality of actions among all Buddhas]:

> When cause, support, function, intention, and endeavor differ, then it is true that there results a difference of action in the world; but because these five differences do not obtain for Buddhas, the actions of the World-protectors are identical.

32. If the Dharma body of Buddhas, possessing these many good qualities and such perfections, is not common to word-hearers and solitary enlightened ones, then with what intention has [the Buddha] taught that they also should journey in a single vehicle, i.e., the Buddha vehicle? Here are stanzas on this point:

> [The Buddha] has taught a single vehicle to lead word-hearers

> of undetermined [lineage], other bodhisattvas [of undetermined lineage], and [bodhisattvas] of determined lineage into the Great Vehicle.
>
> He taught a single vehicle because of the identity of reality, of non-self, and of liberation; because of the differences of lineage; because of the acquisition of cessation in two aspirations; and because of ultimacy.

33. If all Buddhas in the triple world possess the same Dharma body, then how can we enumerate different Buddhas? Here is a stanza on this point:

> Because in one realm there are not two [Buddhas], [but] because innumerable [bodhisattvas] simultaneously complete [their] causal practices, and because a sequential realization of Buddhahood is impossible, therefore one can validly affirm that there are many different Buddhas at the same time.

34. How is it that Buddhas have neither entered final cessation nor not entered final cessation in the Dharma body? Here is a stanza:

> Because they are liberated from all obstacles, and since their action is without end, Buddhas both enter final cessation and do not enter final cessation.

35. Why is the enjoyment body not the essence body? There are six reasons: 1) because [the enjoyment body] appears as a material body and as an activated body; 2) because it appears differently among the innumerable great assemblies; 3) because, being seen in accordance with the aspirations [of sentient beings], it manifests fundamental differences; 4) because, being seen in a variety of different ways, it appears as fundamentally changeable; 5) because, being related to a variety of assemblies, those of bodhisattvas, word-hearers, gods, and so forth, it is relational; and 6) because of the [dissimilar] appearance of the two conversions of support of the container consciousness and of the active

consciousnesses. It is therefore not reasonable that the enjoyment body be identified with the essence body.

36. Why is the transformation body not the essence body? There are eight reasons: 1) it is not possible that a bodhisattva who has long since obtained irreversible concentrations should be born in the Tuṣita [Heaven] or among men; 2) it is not possible that one who has [long since] remembered his [previous] rebirths should not have complete understanding of writing, calculation, mathematics, illustrating, crafts, scholarship, and the enjoyment of and indulgence in sensual desire; 3) it is not possible that one who [long since] has 132b
understood the difference between good and bad presentations of doctrine should go to heretics and take them as his teachers; 4) it is not possible that a bodhisattva who long since has understood the validity of the noble paths of the three vehicles should have engaged in useless austerities in searching for the path; 5) it is not possible that, upon leaving behind a hundred millions of Jambudvīpas, [a bodhisattva] should realize complete awakening and set in motion the wheel of doctrine at a single location; 6) if, without manifesting the skillful means of complete awakening, [a bodhisattva] were to perform the action of a Buddha in the other [Jambudvīpas] by means of transformation bodies, then he might also attain complete awakening in the Tuṣita [Heaven]; 7) if this is not so, then why did the Buddha not appear equally in all the Jambudvīpas [at the same time]? Why did he not appear in other places? No scripture or reasoning invalidates this [assertion]; and 8) [the doctrine of] a multiplicity of transformation bodies does not contradict [the scripture that says that] two Tathāgatas do not arise in [the same] world, since the term world realm [in that scripture] indicates the four continents [of a single Jambudvīpa and not the trichiliocosm]. It is like the impossibility of two universal monarchs (*cakravartins*) arising together in a single world realm. Here is a stanza on this subject:

> The subtle transformation bodies of Buddhas in an identical manner enter into many wombs in order to manifest the awakening of all aspects to the world.

38. There are six reasons why the World-honored Buddhas do not remain permanently in transformation bodies: 1) because of the completion of their actions, since they have finished delivering and maturing [the sentient beings whom they were to deliver and mature]; 2) to cause those who are already liberated and who desire cessation to abandon this aspiration for cessation in seeking to attain an eternal Buddha body; 3) to eradicate disrespect toward the Buddha and engender an understanding of the profound reality of true suchness and the enunciated doctrine; 4) to arouse longing [for the Buddha], lest those who see him continually take him for granted; 5) so that [beings] might themselves develop zeal, knowing that the True Teacher cannot be found; and 6) to cause them quickly to reach maturity by not abandoning their own zealous efforts for the task. Here is a stanza on this point:

> Because their actions are complete, to avoid desire for cessation, to eradicate disrespect toward the Buddha, to arouse longing [for the Buddha], to bring about their own zeal, and quickly to attain maturity, it is impossible for the Buddha permanently to abide in transformation bodies.[23]

132c 36. In order to deliver all sentient beings, [Buddhas] seek supreme awakening through their vows and practices. Complete, final cessation is thus impossible [for them], because that would render those vows and practices inefficacious.

37. Since neither the enjoyment body nor the transformation body is eternal, how can it be said [in the scriptures] that the Tathāgata's body is eternal? Because both the apparitional body and the transformation body are supported upon the eternal Dharma body, because the apparitional body is never abandoned, and because the transformation [body] shows itself again and again. It is like the expressions: "He always experiences happiness," or "He always gives food (i.e., alms)." These two bodies should be understood in this fashion.

39. Although the Dharma body of Buddhas is beginningless, not distinct [from sentient beings], and infinite, it is not appropriate to

fail in effort in order to attain the Dharma body. Here is a stanza on this point:

> The realization and attainment of all Buddhas are identical and infinite. If this causes sentient beings to abandon effort, then this realization and attainment would be forever without cause, but it is impossible to discard the true cause.

Among the collected scriptures of the Great Vehicle Abhidharma, [this text] is called the *Summary of the Great Vehicle*. This true explanation is completed.

Notes

1 Paramārtha, one of four translators of the *Summary of the Great Vehicle* (*Mahāyānasaṃgraha*) into Chinese, is crucially important not merely as a textual witness to Asaṅga's basic text but also as an advocate of the teaching of pure consciousness. In his other works, he teaches that the structure of consciousness is grounded on *"amala-vijñāna,"* i.e., pure consciousness. Paramārtha evidently favored Tathāgatagarbha teachings. Indeed, he appends the concluding verses from the principal Tathāgatagarbha treatise, the *Treatise on the Jeweled Nature* (*Ratnagotra-vibhāga*), to his translation of Vasubandhu's *Commentary on the Summary of the Great Vehicle* (*Mahāyānasaṃgraha-bhāṣya*). Paramārtha lends support to Chinese notions of one's "original enlightenment" or "basic nature," ideas with strong Taoist antecedents. His translation of the *Mahāyānasaṃgraha* is important not only because it is one witness to an ancient Indian treatise but also because it is formative of a host of later Chinese treatises in a number of Chinese schools of Buddhism. At times Paramārtha may be idiosyncratic, and when he is so, I have tried to the best of my ability to reflect his understandings, without homogenizing his Chinese into what we know from the Tibetan or the other three Chinese translations.

2 The other translations refer to an unknown text, the *"Abhidharma-mahāyāna-sūtra,"* as the source for the present stanza. Paramārtha is not so clear, saying literally, "this is the teaching of the Abhidharma and the scriptures of the Great Vehicle," which parataxis I take to mean an Abhidharma-like (i.e., systematic) teaching about the sutras of the Great Vehicle.

3 In broader terms perhaps, the text treats: 1) the structure of mind that supports knowing (Chapter I), 2) the three patterns of knowing in which it can function (Chapter II), 3) the critical theory of conscious construction-only whereby one truly understands that knowing (Chapter III), 4) the path of practice that leads toward the conversion that results in such understanding (Chapters IV to VIII), and 5) the final result of awakening (Chapters IX and X).

4 These ten constitute the systematic treatment of the following ten chapters.

5 Here again the other translations refer to a specific sutra, while Paramārtha attributes the stanza to "the basic or root verses that summarize the Abhidharma."

[6] This is the famous verse from the *Scripture on the Explication of Underlying Meaning* (*Saṃdhinirmocana-sūtra*), chapter 5, section 7. A slightly different version of it appears at the bottom of page 29 of the BDK English Tripiṭaka edition of this sutra, translated by John P. Keenan (Berkeley, CA: Numata Center, 2000).

[7] Note that here the bodhisattvas are taught to understand understanding—in modern parlance, to embrace a critical understanding of mind in order benefit sentient beings. The recommendation is for a hermeneutical approach grounded in critical theory.

[8] Here this deep understanding of dependent co-arising found in the Yogācāra understanding of mind is also the profound teaching of emptiness, for the mind—itself empty—distinguishes and engenders ideas of essences.

[9] Thus, this *Summary of the Great Vehicle* admits no immanently or originally pure mind, for the world-transcendent mind is elicited from hearing teachings that flow from the reality of awakened Buddhas.

[10] Yogācāra shares the Abhidharma teaching that our actions (karma) bring about the very world we inhabit, the world that receives us, but regards that action as mental action engendered by constructs of consciousness. Perhaps every attempt at critical philosophy tends to flirt with or even adopt idealist positions, because it abandons the naive realism of an inner subject looking at outer objects and turns to an examination of the structure and functioning of sensation, understanding, and judgment. There is an argument whether Yogācāra itself simply flirts with or embraces such a position, for often passages negate the reality of external objects, while many other passages speak of knowing reality just as it is.

[11] Note how dominant a role Yogācāra philosophy assigns to language in the conscious construction of the other-dependent pattern (*paratantra*), i.e., the basic pattern of our conscious life, regularly mistaken as imagined realities out there for our pleasure or pain, but recoverable by a conversion of support to the perfected pattern (*parinispanna*).

[12] Paramārtha uses the term "reality" pattern where the other translators speak of the "perfected" pattern (*parinispanna*).

[13] A slightly different version of this passage appears on page 53 of the BDK English Tripiṭaka edition of the *Scripture of the Explication of Underlying Meaning* (see note 6, above).

[14] Note how here Yogācāra employs as elsewhere its critical theory of the three patterns of consciousness (including understanding) to interpret the earlier Prajñāpāramitā teachings.

[15] At issue, perhaps, is how one is to understand the reality pattern. Imagined

states are declared nonexistent, other-dependent stages understood on analogy with fleeting realities, but the perfected reality pattern by means of the perfections of these four purities. How is one to understand "original purity"? Perhaps as the original potential of sentient beings to respond to teaching. Perhaps as the seed of awakening (*tathāgatagarbha*). Paramārtha, in his translation of "original, essential purity," perhaps favors the latter understanding.

16 This is explicit hermeneutical advice: Read the doctrine of the scriptures within the framework of the three patterns of Yogācāra critical theory. This philosophy is not therefore a philosophical notion that parallels earlier Mahayana thinking, as does Mādhyamika thought, but is first and foremost a method for exegesis.

17 In this section, the entire hermeneutic is outlined: First, understand the structure of mind and how language permeates it; then how it functions in the three patterns that arise in dependence on that structure; and finally, apply that understanding of consciousness to the interpretation of the scriptures, as exemplified in the next two sections, 33 and 34, where given scriptural terms are read in terms of later commentaries. These two examples are not very exciting perhaps, and it may be difficult to discern the import of the critical hermeneutic, but perhaps it is enough for the Yogācāra scholar to inculcate the principle, which can then be applied with vigor and zest to other, more controversial readings.

18 It is noteworthy that initial insight, i.e., entry into the features of the knowable, is performed not by some wordless concentration but by "correct reflection" into doctrine. Yogācāra is philosophy based on the practices of yogic concentration but not simply wordless wonder.

19 Even the critical philosophy of Yogācāra is abandoned in nonimaginative wisdom, for without images there is no insight, and without insight no critical philosophy at all. This is perhaps a Yogācāra version of the Mādhyamika maxim that one must see the emptiness even of emptiness.

20 The *Ornament of the Scriptures of the Great Vehicle* (*Mahāyānasūtrālaṃkāra*) is the most frequently cited authority in Asaṅga's *Summary*. Especially frequent are the many citations in chapter ten on awakening as the term of all practice.

21 This is a classic issue in Western theology, "the problem of evil." How can such suffering and evil exist if God is all-powerful and all-loving? Here the terms are different but the structure is parallel: How can bodhisattvas, so powerful and capable of alleviating poverty and suffering, so compassionate and kind toward sentient beings, not actually do so—that is, eliminate poverty and suffering? The answer here echoes one Western response: Bodhisattvas are functioning from a higher perspective and here see the

full unfolding of possible future karmic results, and so even though they may not alleviate present pain and suffering, they are nonetheless acting for the true, although unseen, benefit of sentient beings.

[22] Literally, "the six times." The *Treatise on the Stages of Yogic Meditation* (*Yogācārabhūmi,* Taishō Vol. 30, No. 1579, p. 499b), has: "Thus the Tathāgata of the six times—the three [divisions] of day and the three [divisions] of night—by means of his Buddha-eye, constantly perceives the world."

[23] Paramārtha's order of the remaining sections differs from the other translations. I have enumerated them as they are found in Lamotte's *La Somme du Grand Véhicule d'Asaṇga* to highlight the textual differences. In his translation of Vasubandhu's *Commentary on the Summary of the Great Vehicle* Paramārtha adds stanzas taken from the *Treatise on the Jeweled Nature,* the principle commentary of the Tathāgatagarbha tradition. Perhaps Paramārtha wants readers to understand Yogācāra exclusively in terms of the the Tathāgatagarbha lineage. See Griffiths, et al., *The Realm of Awakening,* pp. 272–3.

Glossary

Abhidharma: Philosophical analysis. Specifically, texts so named which attempt systematic understanding of the Buddha's teaching, commenting on it and arranging it into analytic categories. More generallly, any analytic commentary. Early Mahayana scriptures refute the realism of earlier Abhidharma theory. Later Mahayana thinkers—such as Yogācāra philosophers—reclaim theory in a context of conventional discourse, e.g., the *Treatise on the Stages of Yogic Meditation* (*Yogācārabhūmi*). Asaṅga wrote a glossary entitled *Abhidharma-samuccaya* (*Compendium of Abhidharma Terms*).

Abhidharma Scripture (*Abhidharma-mahāyāna-sūtra*): An early Yogācāra text preserved only in fragments. *See also* Yogācāra.

active consciousnesses (*pravṛtti-vijñāna*): The seven consciousnesses of thinking, perceiving, and the fivefold sense consciousnesses, to be distinguished from the latent container consciousness. *See also* container consciousness; perceiving consciousness; sense consciousnesses; thinking consciousness.

Analysis of the Middle and the Extremes (*Madhyānta-vibhāga*): A Yogācāra text attributed to Maitreya.

appropriating consciousness (*ādāna-vijñāna*): The consciousness that appropriates the sense body and supports transmigration; a synonym for the container consciousness. *See also* container consciousness; transmigration.

Asaṅga (ca. 310–390 C.E.): With his brother Vasubandhu, co-founder of the School of Conscious Construction-only (Vijñaptimātratā), also known as the Yogācāra; author of the *Summary of the Great Vehicle* (*Mahāyāna-saṃgraha*). *See also* Vasubandhu; Yogācāra.

asura: A class of superhuman beings that are in constant conflict with the gods.

Asvabhāva (ca. sixth century C.E.): Author of the *Interpretation of the Summary of the Great Vehicle* (*Mahāyānasaṃgrahopanibandhana*).

bodhisattva ("enlightenment being"): The spiritual ideal of the Mahayana, a selfless being with universal compassion who sees the universal emptiness of phenomena and has generated the profound aspiration to achieve enlightenment in order to benefit sentient beings. In the course of their spiritual careers, bodhisattvas engage in the practice of the six perfections and pass through ten stages of increasingly higher levels of spiritual accomplishment. *See also* emptiness; Mahayana; six perfections; ten stages.

Bodhisattva Stages (*Bodhisattvabhūmi*): A basic Mahayana text.

Buddha factors: Six factors that comprise the Dharma body—purification, maturation, dwelling, mastery, verbal expression, and alleviation.

Buddha-nature: The basic enlightened nature of sentient beings, which is chronically obscured by their ignorance. The complete unfolding of the Buddha-nature is enlightenment itself.

concentration (*samādhi, samāpatti*): Any of various states of meditative absorption, each characterized by different qualities. Nonconceptual concentration (*nirvikalpa-samāpatti*) is fundamental wisdom, apart from any content but poised to reengage in a dependently co-arisen world. The concentration of destruction (*nirodha-samāpatti*), by contrast, is a transient state that suspends all mental activity whatsoever.

condition (*pratyaya*): The entity whereby something comes to be. The Yogācāra posits a fourfold schema of conditions: the direct cause (*hetu-pratyaya*); the dominant condition (*adhipati-pratyaya*), which leads a direct cause to exercise its efficacy; the immediately antecedent condition (*samanantara-pratyaya*), whereby, in a constant state of momentariness, the instantaneous state of a thing causes its immediately subsequent state; and the objective cause (*ālambana-pratyaya*), the object that causes a corresponding consciousness to arise. Yogācāra thinkers inherited this schema from Abhidharma philosophy.

conscious construction-only (*vijñapti-mātratā*): The central teaching of the Yogācāra school of Buddhism, which indicates that we mistakenly take mental constructions (*vijñapti*) as presenting realities external to the consciousness (*vijñāna*) in which they appear, yet they are only mental constructs and not ultimate truth. *See also* Yogācāra.

container consciousness (*ālaya-vijñāna*): The latent, seminal consciousness that supports karmically defiled awareness; the storehouse of all the seeds, imprints of mental defilements, that generate delusion. *See also* seed.

conversion of support (*āśraya-parāvṛtti*): Refers to the conversion, or turning around of consciousness from the imagined (*parikalpita*) to the reality pattern (*parinispanna*). *See also* imagined pattern; reality pattern.

correct reflection (*yoniśo-manaskāra*): Insight into the mental words of doctrine.

defiled and pure aspect: A term used in the *Abhidharma Scripture* for the other-dependent pattern (*paratantra*). *See also* other-dependent pattern.

defiled aspect: A term used in the *Abhidharma Scripture* for an imagined pattern (*parikalpita*). *See also* imagined pattern.

dependent co-arising (*pratītyasamutpāda*): The doctrine that all things come into being only in dependence upon other things; mutual causality between things; in this text it refers to the mutual causality between the different levels of consciousness.

destiny (*gati*): Any of the six realms of existence in which sentient beings are born in the cycle of transmigration—the realms of the gods (*devas*), angry titans (*asuras*), humans, animals, hungry ghosts (*pretas*), or hell (*naraka*). Birth in these various destinies is conditioned on one's karmic past. *See also* transmigration.

deva: A god; a divine being.

Dharma body (*dharmakāya*): The sphere of ultimate reality characterized by the conversion of support, by radiant qualities, by nonduality, by eternity, and by inconceivability. *See also* three bodies.

emptiness (*śūnyatā*): The absence of permanent essence in things. All phenomena are devoid of independent, permanent existence, self-nature (*svabhāva*), and instead exist only in dependence on a complex web of causes and conditions and go on existing only as long as those causes and conditions prevail. The doctrine of emptiness is the central teaching of Mahayana Buddhism. In Yogācāra philosophy, the term is used to refer to the absence of the imagined pattern in the other-dependent pattern. *See also* imagined pattern; Mahayana; other-dependent pattern; Yogācāra.

enjoyment body (*saṃbhogakāya*): An apparent material or activated body supported on the Dharma body and appearing for the sake of bodhisattvas. *See also* bodhisattva; Dharma body; three bodies.

eon (*kalpa*): An immeasurably long period of time, thought to be necessary to uproot one's karmic past by the practice of the path.

essence body (*svābhāvikakāya*): Same as the Dharma body. *See also* Dharma body.

evolutions of consciousness (*vijñāna-pariṇāma*): The karmic developments of consciousness.

experiential consciousness: The active consciousness of sense experience, discrimination, and activity.

foundational consciousness (*mūla-vijñāna*): Synonym for the container consciousness, foundational because it is the latent source of karmic conditioning for the active consciousnesses. *See also* active consciousnesses; container consciousness.

four inquiries: Four correct doctrinal insights into names, objects, essences, and differences.

four intentions and four aims: The intentions and aims of Buddhas, according to which one must interpret scripture.

four kinds of birth: According to Buddhism, the four possible ways that a being may be born, i.e., 1) from a womb, 2) from an egg, 3) from moisture, or 4) through metamorphosis or spontaneous generation.

four kinds of pure states: Original purity, undefiled purity, purity of path, and purity of object.

four wisdoms: The four types of transformed consciousness discussed in Yogācāra philosophy—1) clear manifestation (*ādarśa-jñāna*), 2) equality (*samatā-jñāna*), 3) returning insight (*pratyavekṣaṇā-jñāna*), and 4) duty fulfillment (*kṛtyānuṣṭhāna-jñāna*). These wisdoms emerge from the eight forms of consciousness when illusion is destroyed and enlightenment is realized. *See also* Yogācāra.

garuḍa: A mythological being in the form of a giant bird.

Hinayana ("Lesser Vehicle): A generic term applied by Mahayanists to the vehicles of the word-hearers and the solitary enlightened ones, characterized by insight into emptiness of self but not the emptiness of things. *See also* emptiness; Mahayana; solitary enlightened one; word-hearer.

Hui-k'ai (517–568): Paramārtha's disciple and amanuensis.

imagined pattern (*parikalpita-svabhāva*): The appearance of nonexistent objects, which are only conscious constructs, as real.

kiṃnara: A class of mythical beings, either half human and half bird or half human and half horse, that make celestial music.

Mādhyamika: Nāgārjuna's philosophy of the Middle Way, explaining emptiness. *See also* Nāgārjuna.

Mahayana ("Great Vehicle"): A form of Buddhism that developed in India around 100 B.C.E. and which exalts as its religious ideal bodhisattvas, great beings who are willing to delay their own enlightenment until they can save all sentient beings. Such selfless compassion becomes possible only when the practitioner grasps the central Mahayana doctrine of emptiness. *See also* bodhisattva; emptiness.

mahoraga: A class of snake-like mythical beings.

masteries: Five masteries of the Dharma body—in manifesting Buddha lands, over pleasant abodes, in teaching, in transformations, and in the four wisdoms. *See also* Dharma body.

maturing consciousnesses (*vipāka-vijñāna*): The basic character of the container consciousness permeated by karmic seeds. *See also* container consciousness; seed.

mind (*citta*): A synonym for the container consciousness. *See also* container consciousness.

Nāgārjuna (second–third century B.C.E.): The principal philosopher of the Mahayana teaching of emptiness. *See also* emptiness; Mahayana.

non-abiding cessation (*apratiṣṭhita-nirvāṇa*): Bodhisattvas' attainment of cessation whereby they abandon defilement but not transmigration. *See also* bodhisattva; transmigration.

nonimaginative wisdom (*nirvikalpa-jñāna*): Nondiscriminative wisdom; wisdom apart from any image, concept, or judgment that might distinguish or discriminate one thing from another. Silent, wordless wisdom.

original purity (*prakṛti-vyavadāna*): Essential purity, suchness, the reality limit, the imageless, reality, the reality realm.

Ornament of the Sutra of the Great Vehicle (*Mahāyānasūtrālaṃkāra*): A basic Yogācāra text attributed to Maitreya. *See also* Yogācāra.

other-dependent pattern (*paratantra-svabhāva*): The consciously constructed differentiations that have the container consciousness as their seed and that are included within unreal imagining. *See also* container consciousness.

outflow from the pure reality realm (*dharmadhātu-niṣyanda*): A characterization of the purity of object, i.e., the doctrine, as coming directly from the realm of reality.

Paramārtha (499–569): One of the four Chinese translators of the *Summary of the Great Vehicle.*

perceiving consciousness (*manovijñāna*): The mind that perceives that which has been contacted through a sense organ and its corresponding sense consciousness. *See also* sense consciousnesses.

perfection (*pāramitā*): The Mahayana understanding of wisdom and virtue, perfected by insight into emptiness to go beyond the previous attachment to "good works." *See also* Mahayana.

permeation (*vāsanā*): The influence of karmic seeds upon consciousness. *See also* seed.

permeation of hearing (*śruta-vāsanā*): The imbuing of the mind with the hearing of doctrine.

Prajñāpāramitā ("Perfection of Wisdom"): The name of a body of Mahayana scriptures that emphasize the doctrine of emptiness, and which served as the fundamental texts for a number of important Buddhist schools, including Yogācāra. *See also* emptiness; Mahayana; Yogācāra.

primal ignorance (*avidyā*): The unenlightened state.

pure aspect: A term in the *Abhidharma Scripture* for the reality pattern (*pariniṣpanna*). *See also* reality pattern.

purity of object (*ālambana-vyavadāna*): The true doctrine of the Great Vehicle (Mahayana), which is the object of teaching and meditation.

purity of path (*mārga-vyavadāna*): The path of practice leading to undefiled purity.

quietude and insight (*śamatha-vipaśyanā*): The two traditional phases of meditative concentration. *See also* concentration.

reality pattern (*pariniṣpanna-svabhāva*): The eternal nonexistence in the other-dependent pattern of nonexistent objects. *See also* other-dependent pattern.

saint (arhat): An accomplished practitioner, the highest degree of spiritual attainment in the Hinayana. While the term sometimes comes under criticism by Mahayana thinkers as exemplifying an inferior practitioner, it is often applied to Buddhas and bodhisattvas, no doubt due to the force of the ancient traditions. *See also* Hinayana; Mahayana.

Scripture on the Explication of Underlying Meaning (*Saṃdhinirmocana-sūtra*): A foundational Yogācāra scripture. *See also* Yogācāra.

seed (*bīja*): The inner habit energies that lie in the container consciousness. *See also* container consciousness.

sense consciousnesses: The consciousnesses, i.e., visual consciousness, aural consciousness, olfactory consciousness, gustatory consciousness, and tactile consciousness, that arise from contact between the five sense organs of the eyes, ears, nose, tongue, and body with their respective objects.

single vehicle (*ekayāna*): The one Buddha vehicle of the Mahayana. *See also* Mahayana.

six perfections (*parāmitā*s): The traditional six bodhisattva virtues—giving (*dāna*), discipline (*śīla*), patience (*kṣānti*), zeal (*vīrya*), meditation (*dhyāna*), and wisdom (*prajñā*).

solitary enlightened one (*pratyekabuddha*): A sage who attains enlightenment by directly observing the dependent co-arising of phenomena, without the guidance of a teacher, and who intends neither to guide others nor to expound the teaching to others. One of the two kinds of Hinayana sages. *See also* dependent co-arising; Hinayana.

subsequently attained wisdom (*pṛṣṭhalabdha-jñāna*): Correct discriminative wisdom realized after nonimaginative wisdom, in virtue of which a bodhisattva carries out the tasks of compassion. *See also* bodhisattva; nonimaginative wisdom.

suchness (*tathatā*): The content of wisdom insight into things as they really are; ultimate truth; ultimate reality. The content of the perfect wisdom (*prajñāpāramitā*) insight into the nature of reality just as it is, i.e., empty of self-nature and dependently arisen. Apprehension of this state is enlightenment. *See also* dependent co-arising; emptiness.

Tathāgata: An epithet for the Buddha. It means "one who has gone to (*gata*) and come from (*āgata*) the truth of suchness (*tathā*)," i.e., "one who embodies the truth of suchness (*tathā*)." *See also* suchness.

tathāgatagarbha: Another name for the Buddha-nature that is within all beings, conceived of as a kind of storeroom or receptacle where the embryo of the Tathāgata is retained and matured. *See also* Buddha-nature; Tathāgata.

ten distractions: The varieties of distracted imaginings that must be countered by nonimaginative wisdom. *See also* nonimaginative wisdom.

ten stages: The stages (*bhūmis*) of bodhisattva practice—joy (*pramuditā-bhūmi*), stainlessness (*vimalā-bhūmi*), bright radiance (*prabhākarī-bhūmi*), blazing fire (*arciṣmatī-bhūmi*), difficult to conquer (*sudurjayā-bhūmi*), presence (*abhimukhī-bhūmi*), far-reaching (*dūraṃgamā-bhūmi*), imperturbability (*acalā-bhūmi*), subtle wisdom (*sādhumatī-bhūmi*), and the Dharma cloud (*dharmameghā-bhūmi*). *See also* bodhisattva.

thinking consciousness: Each of the sense organs, including the perceiving mind, has a corresponding consciousness by which its objects are known. The thinking function of the mind arises from and leads to defilement by giving rise to discriminative thoughts and false ideas. *See also* container consciousness; perceiving consciousness; sense consciousnesses.

thought (*manas*): This term comprises both the immediately disappearing consciousness and defiled thinking.

three bodies (*trikāya*): The three bodies of the Buddha—1) the Dharma body (*dharmakāya*), which is the Buddha as suchness or ultimate reality, 2) the enjoyment body (*saṃbhogakāya*), acquired by Buddhas through absolute perfection of their practice; this body can go everywhere, is omniscient, etc., and 3) the transformation body (*nirmāṇakāya*), whereby, out of compassion, the Buddha manifests in an infinite number of forms in order to assist sentient beings. *See also* suchness.

three patterns (*trisvabhāva*): The three modes of consciousness—imagination (*parikalpita*), other-dependence (*paratantra*), and reality (*pariniṣpanna*). *See also* imagined pattern; other-dependent pattern; reality pattern.

three themes: The summary themes of the Great Vehicle (i.e., the Mahayana) according to Yogācāra philosophy—the dependent co-arising of the consciousnesses; dependently co-arisen states or the active evolutions of consciousness; and the meaning of what has been taught, i.e., a hermeneutic drawn from Yogācāra critical theory. *See also* Mahayana; Yogācāra.

three vehicles: The paths of the word-hearers, solitary enlightened ones, and bodhisattvas, respectively. *See also* bodhisattva; solitary enlightened one; word-hearer.

transformation body (*nirmāṇakāya*): A fictive body supported on the Dharma body and appearing for the sake of word-hearers and solitary enlightened ones. *See also* Dharma body; solitary enlightened one; three bodies; word-hearer.

transmigration (samsara): The cycle of birth, death, and rebirth to which sentient beings are subject as a result of their past actions (karma). *See also* destiny.

triple word: 1) The world of desire (*kāmadhātu*), 2) the world of form (*rūpa-dhātu*), experienced by those who have severed all desires but still experience the world as form, and 3) the world of formlessness (*ārūpyadhātu*), experienced by those who have severed all desires and attachment to form but have still not attained enlightenment.

two vehicles: The two Hinayana paths of the word-hearers and solitary enlightened ones. *See also* Hinayana; solitary enlightened one; word-hearer.

undefiled purity (*vaimālya-vyavadāna*): Original purity separated from all adventitious defilements.

Vasubandhu (ca. 320–400 C.E.): The brother of Asaṅga and co-founder of the School of Conscious Construction-only (Vijñaptimātratā), also known as the Yogācāra; author of the *Commentary on the Summary of the Great Vehicle* (*Mahāyānasaṃgraha-bhāṣya*). *See also* Asaṅga; Yogācāra.

wisdom of omniscience (*sarvajñā*): The all-knowing wisdom of a bodhisattva. *See also* bodhisattva.

word-hearer (*śrāvaka*): Originally, a disciple of the Buddha, one who directly heard his teachings; a practitioner who follows a literal interpretation of scripture; later generally used by Mahayanists to refer to followers of the Hinayana. *See also* Hinayana; Mahayana.

yakṣa: A class of demonic beings.

Yogācāra: Literally, the practice of meditative union (*yoga*); an alternate name for the School of Conscious Construction-only (Vijñaptimātratā) developed by the Indian masters Asaṅga and Vasubandhu in the fourth century C.E.. The name may indicate that the original members of this school focused on practices of yogic meditation. *See also* Asaṅga; conscious construction-only; Vasubandhu.

Bibliography

Anacker, Stefan. *Seven Works of Vasubandhu, the Buddhist Psychological Doctor*. Delhi: Motilal Banarsidass, 1984.

Griffiths, Paul J. *On Being Mindless: Buddhist Meditation and the Mind-Body Problem*. LaSalle, IL: Open Court, 1986.

Griffiths, Paul J., Noriaki Hakamaya, John P. Keenan, and Paul Swanson. *The Realm of Awakening: Chapter Ten of Asaṅga's Mahāyāna-saṃgraha*. New York and Oxford: Oxford University Press, 1989.

Hakamaya, Noriaki. "The Realm of Enlightenment in Vijñaptimātratā: The Formulation of the Four Kinds of Pure Dharmas." *Journal of the International Association of Buddhist Studies* 3 (1980): 21–41.

Hall, Bruce Cameron. "The Meaning of Vijñapti in Vasubandhu's Concept of Mind." *Journal of the International Association of Buddhist Studies* 9 (1986): 7–23.

Hattori, Masaaki. "The Transformation of the Basis (*āśraya-parāvṛtti*) in the Yogācāra System of Philosophy." In *All-Einheit: Wege eines Gedankens in Ost und West,* edited by Dietrich Heinrich, pp. 100–8. Stuttgart: Klett-Cotta, 1981.

Keenan, John P. "Original Purity and the Focus of Early Yogācāra." *Journal of the International Association of Buddhist Studies* 5 (1982): 7–18.

—. "Pure Land Systematics in India: The Buddhabhūmisūtra and the Trikāya Doctrine." *Pacific World* 3 (1987): 29–35.

Lamotte, Étienne. *La Somme du Grand Véhicule d'Asaṅga (Mahāyāna-saṃgraha)*. 2 vols. Louvain-la-Neuve: Institut Orientaliste, Université de Louvain, 1973. This French translation is the standard Western-language translation of the *Summary of the Great Vehicle.*

Lindtner, Christian. "A Treatise on Buddhist Idealism: Kambala's Alokamala." In *Miscellanea Buddhica,* edited by Christian Lindtner, pp. 109–221. Copenhagen: Akademisk Forlag, 1985.

Nagao, Gadjin. *The Foundational Standpoint of Mādhyamika Philosoph* Translated by John P. Keenan. Albany, NY: State University of Ne York Press, 1989.

—. *Shōdaijōron: Wayaku to chūkai* (*Summary of the Great Vehicle:* Japa ese Translation and Notes). 2 vols. Tokyo: Kodansha, 1982 and 198 Japanese translation based on all four Chinese translations and Tibet translation. Sanskrit reconstruction appended. The standard stud

—. *Mādhyamika and Yogācāra: A Study of Mahāyāna Philosophies: Co lected Papers of G. M. Nagao*. Edited, collated, and translated by L. Kawamura in collaboration with G. M. Nagao. Albany, NY: State Un versity of New York Press, 1991.

Paul, Diana. *Philosophy of Mind in Sixth-Century China: Paramārtha "Evolution of Consciousness."* Palo Alto, CA: Stanford University Pres 1984. A well-researched and readable book on Paramārtha and h thought.

Schmithausen, Lambert. *Ālayavijñāna: On the Origin and Early Develop ment of a Central Concept in Yogācāra Buddhism*. 2 vols. Tokyo: Inte national Institute for Buddhist Studies, 1987.

Tatz, Mark. *Asaṅga's Chapter on Ethics with the Commentary of Tsong Khapa, the Basic Path to Awakening, the Complete Bodhisattva*. Lewis ton, NY: Edwin Mellen Press, 1986.

Index

B

C

E

F

N

O

P

A List of the Volumes of the BDK English Tripiṭaka
(First Series)

Abbreviations

Ch.: Chinese
Skt.: Sanskrit
Jp.: Japanese
Eng.: Published title
T.: Taishō Tripiṭaka

Vol. No.		Title	*T.* No.
1, 2	*Ch.*	Ch'ang-a-han-ching (長阿含經)	1
	Skt.	Dīrghāgama	
3–8	*Ch.*	Chung-a-han-ching (中阿含經)	26
	Skt.	Madhyamāgama	
9-I	*Ch.*	Ta-ch'eng-pên-shêng-hsin-ti-kuan-ching (大乘本生心地觀經)	159
9-II	*Ch.*	Fo-so-hsing-tsan (佛所行讃)	192
	Skt.	Buddhacarita	
10-I	*Ch.*	Tsa-pao-ts'ang-ching (雜寶藏經)	203
	Eng.	The Storehouse of Sundry Valuables	
10-II	*Ch.*	Fa-chü-p'i-yü-ching (法句譬喩經)	211
	Eng.	The Scriptural Text: Verses of the Doctrine, with Parables	
11-I	*Ch.*	Hsiao-p'in-pan-jo-po-lo-mi-ching (小品般若波羅蜜經)	227
	Skt.	Aṣṭasāhasrikā-prajñāpāramitā-sūtra	
11-II	*Ch.*	Chin-kang-pan-jo-po-lo-mi-ching (金剛般若波羅蜜經)	235
	Skt.	Vajracchedikā-prajñāpāramitā-sūtra	

Vol. No.		Title	T. No.
11-III	*Ch.*	Jên-wang-pan-jo-po-lo-mi-ching (仁王般若波羅蜜經)	245
	Skt.	Kāruṇikārājā-prajñāpāramitā-sūtra (?)	
11-IV	*Ch.*	Pan-jo-po-lo-mi-to-hsing-ching (般若波羅蜜多心經)	251
	Skt.	Prajñāpāramitāhṛdaya-sūtra	
12-I	*Ch.*	Ta-lo-chin-kang-pu-k'ung-chên-shih-san-mo-yeh-ching (大樂金剛不空眞實三麼耶經)	243
	Skt.	Adhyardhaśatikā-prajñāpāramitā-sūtra	
12-II	*Ch.*	Wu-liang-shou-ching (無量壽經)	360
	Skt.	Sukhāvatīvyūha	
	Eng.	The Larger Sutra on Amitāyus (In The Three Pure Land Sutras)	
12-III	*Ch.*	Kuan-wu-liang-shou-fo-ching (觀無量壽佛經)	365
	Skt.	Amitāyurdhyāna-sūtra	
	Eng.	The Sutra on Contemplation of Amitāyus (In The Three Pure Land Sutras)	
12-IV	*Ch.*	A-mi-t'o-ching (阿彌陀經)	366
	Skt.	Sukhāvatīvyūha	
	Eng.	The Smaller Sutra on Amitāyus (In The Three Pure Land Sutras)	
12-V	*Ch.*	Ti-ts'ang-p'u-sa-pên-yüan-ching (地藏菩薩本願經)	412
	Skt.	Kṣitigarbhapraṇidhāna-sūtra (?)	
12-VI	*Ch.*	Yao-shih-liu-li-kuang-ju-lai-pên-yüan-kung-tê-ching (藥師琉璃光如來本願功德經)	450
	Skt.	Bhaiṣajyaguruvaiḍūryaprabhāsapūrva-praṇidhānaviśeṣavistara	
12-VII	*Ch.*	Mi-lê-hsia-shêng-ch'êng-fo-ching (彌勒下生成佛經)	454
	Skt.	Maitreyavyākaraṇa (?)	
12-VIII	*Ch.*	Wên-shu-shih-li-wên-ching (文殊師利問經)	468
	Skt.	Mañjuśrīparipṛcchā (?)	
13-I	*Ch.*	Miao-fa-lien-hua-ching (妙法蓮華經)	262
	Skt.	Saddharmapuṇḍarīka-sūtra	
	Eng.	The Lotus Sutra	
13-II	*Ch.*	Wu-liang-i-ching (無量義經)	276

Vol. No.		Title	*T.* No.
13-III	*Ch.*	Kuan-p'u-hsien-p'u-sa-hsing-fa-ching (觀普賢菩薩行法經)	277
14–19	*Ch.*	Ta-fang-kuang-fo-hua-yen-ching (大方廣佛華嚴經)	278
	Skt.	Avataṃsaka-sūtra	
20-I	*Ch.*	Shêng-man-shih-tzŭ-hou-i-ch'eng-ta-fang-pien-fang-kuang-ching (勝鬘師子吼一乘大方便方廣經)	353
	Skt.	Śrīmālādevīsiṃhanāda-sūtra	
20-II	*Ch.*	Chin-kuang-ming-tsui-shêng-wang-ching (金光明最勝王經)	665
	Skt.	Suvarṇaprabhāsa-sūtra	
21–24	*Ch.*	Ta-pan-nieh-p'an-ching (大般涅槃經)	374
	Skt.	Mahāparinirvāṇa-sūtra	
25-I	*Ch.*	Fo-ch'ui-pan-nieh-p'an-liao-shuo-chiao-chieh-ching (佛垂般涅槃略說教誡經)	389
25-II	*Ch.*	Pan-chou-san-mei-ching (般舟三昧經)	418
	Skt.	Pratyutpannabuddhasammukhāvasthitasamādhi-sūtra	
	Eng.	The Pratyutpanna Samādhi Sutra	
25-III	*Ch.*	Shou-lêng-yen-san-mei-ching (首楞嚴三昧經)	642
	Skt.	Śūraṅgamasamādhi-sūtra	
	Eng.	The Śūraṅgama Samādhi Sutra	
25-IV	*Ch.*	Chieh-shên-mi-ching (解深密經)	676
	Skt.	Saṃdhinirmocana-sūtra	
	Eng.	The Scripture on the Explication of Underlying Meaning	
25-V	*Ch.*	Yü-lan-p'ên-ching (盂蘭盆經)	685
	Skt.	Ullambana-sūtra (?)	
25-VI	*Ch.*	Ssŭ-shih-êrh-chang-ching (四十二章經)	784
26-I	*Ch.*	Wei-mo-chieh-so-shuo-ching (維摩詰所說經)	475
	Skt.	Vimalakīrtinirdeśa-sūtra	
26-II	*Ch.*	Yüeh-shang-nü-ching (月上女經)	480
	Skt.	Candrottarādārikāparipṛcchā	

Vol. No.		Title	*T.* No.
26-III	*Ch.*	Tso-ch'an-san-mei-ching (坐禪三昧經)	614
26-IV	*Ch.*	Ta-mo-to-lo-ch'an-ching (達磨多羅禪經)	618
	Skt.	Yogācārabhūmi-sūtra (?)	
27	*Ch.*	Yüeh-têng-san-mei-ching (月燈三昧經)	639
	Skt.	Samādhirājacandrapradīpa-sūtra	
28	*Ch.*	Ju-lêng-ch'ieh-ching (入楞伽經)	671
	Skt.	Laṅkāvatāra-sūtra	
29-I	*Ch.*	Ta-fang-kuang-yüan-chio-hsiu-to-lo-liao-i-ching (大方廣圓覺修多羅了義經)	842
29-II	*Ch.*	Su-hsi-ti-chieh-lo-ching (蘇悉地羯囉經)	893
	Skt.	Susiddhikaramahātantrasādhanopāyika-paṭala	
	Eng.	The Susiddhikara Sutra (In Two Esoteric Sutras)	
29-III	*Ch.*	Mo-têng-ch'ieh-ching (摩登伽經)	1300
	Skt.	Mātaṅgī-sūtra (?)	
30-I	*Ch.*	Ta-p'i-lu-chê-na-chêng-fo-shên-pien-chia-ch'ih-ching (大毘盧遮那成佛神變加持經)	848
	Skt.	Mahāvairocanābhisambodhivikurvitādhiṣṭhāna-vaipulyasūtrendrarāja-nāma-dharmaparyāya	
30-II	*Ch.*	Ching-kang-ting-i-ch'ieh-ju-lai-chên-shih-shê-ta-ch'eng-hsien-chêng-ta-chiao-wang-ching (金剛頂一切如來眞實攝大乘現證大教王經)	865
	Skt.	Sarvatathāgatatattvasaṃgrahamahāyānābhisamayamahākalparāja	
	Eng.	The Adamantine Pinnacle Sutra (In Two Esoteric Sutras)	
31–35	*Ch.*	Mo-ho-sêng-ch'i-lü (摩訶僧祇律)	1425
	Skt.	Mahāsāṃghika-vinaya (?)	
36–42	*Ch.*	Ssŭ-fên-lü (四分律)	1428
	Skt.	Dharmaguptaka-vinaya (?)	
43, 44	*Ch.*	Shan-chien-lü-p'i-p'o-sha (善見律毘婆沙)	1462
	Pāli	Samantapāsādikā	
45-I	*Ch.*	Fan-wang-ching (梵網經)	1484
	Skt.	Brahmajāla-sūtra (?)	

Vol. No.		Title	T. No.
45-II	*Ch.*	Yu-p'o-sai-chieh-ching (優婆塞戒經)	1488
	Skt.	Upāsakaśīla-sūtra (?)	
	Eng.	The Sutra on Upāsaka Precepts	
46-I	*Ch.*	Miao-fa-lien-hua-ching-yu-po-t'i-shê (妙法蓮華經憂波提舍)	1519
	Skt.	Saddharmapuṇḍarīka-upadeśa	
46-II	*Ch.*	Fo-ti-ching-lun (佛地經論)	1530
	Skt.	Buddhabhūmisūtra-śāstra (?)	
	Eng.	The Interpretation of the Buddha Land	
46-III	*Ch.*	Shê-ta-ch'eng-lun (攝大乘論)	1593
	Skt.	Mahāyānasaṃgraha	
	Eng.	The Summary of the Great Vehicle	
47	*Ch.*	Shih-chu-p'i-p'o-sha-lun (十住毘婆沙論)	1521
	Skt.	Daśabhūmika-vibhāṣā (?)	
48, 49	*Ch.*	A-p'i-ta-mo-chü-shê-lun (阿毘達磨俱舍論)	1558
	Skt.	Abhidharmakośa-bhāṣya	
50–59	*Ch.*	Yü-ch'ieh-shih-ti-lun (瑜伽師地論)	1579
	Skt.	Yogācārabhūmi	
60-I	*Ch.*	Ch'êng-wei-shih-lun (成唯識論)	1585
	Eng.	Demonstration of Consciousness Only (In Three Texts on Consciousness Only)	
60-II	*Ch.*	Wei-shih-san-shih-lun-sung (唯識三十論頌)	1586
	Skt.	Triṃśikā	
	Eng.	The Thirty Verses on Consciousness Only (In Three Texts on Consciousness Only)	
60-III	*Ch.*	Wei-shih-êrh-shih-lun (唯識二十論)	1590
	Skt.	Viṃśatikā	
	Eng.	The Treatise in Twenty Verses on Consciousness Only (In Three Texts on Consciousness Only)	
61-I	*Ch.*	Chung-lun (中論)	1564
	Skt.	Madhyamaka-śāstra	
61-II	*Ch.*	Pien-chung-pien-lun (辯中邊論)	1600
	Skt.	Madhyāntavibhāga	

Vol. No.		Title	*T.* No.
61-III	*Ch.* *Skt.*	Ta-ch'eng-ch'êng-yeh-lun (大乘成業論) Karmasiddhiprakaraṇa	1609
61-IV	*Ch.* *Skt.*	Yin-ming-ju-chêng-li-lun (因明入正理論) Nyāyapraveśa	1630
61-V	*Ch.* *Skt.*	Chin-kang-chên-lun (金剛針論) Vajrasūcī	1642
61-VI	*Ch.*	Chang-so-chih-lun (彰所知論)	1645
62	*Ch.* *Skt.*	Ta-ch'eng-chuang-yen-ching-lun (大乘莊嚴經論) Mahāyānasūtrālaṃkāra	1604
63-I	*Ch.* *Skt.*	Chiu-ching-i-ch'eng-pao-hsing-lun (究竟一乘寶性論) Ratnagotravibhāgamahāyānottaratantra-śāstra	1611
63-II	*Ch.* *Skt.*	P'u-t'i-hsing-ching (菩提行經) Bodhicaryāvatāra	1662
63-III	*Ch.*	Chin-kang-ting-yü-ch'ieh-chung-fa-a-nou-to-lo-san-miao-san-p'u-t'i-hsin-lun (金剛頂瑜伽中發阿耨多羅三藐三菩提心論)	1665
63-IV	*Ch.* *Skt.*	Ta-ch'eng-ch'i-hsin-lun (大乘起信論) Mahāyānaśraddhotpāda-śāstra (?)	1666
63-V	*Ch.* *Pāli*	Na-hsien-pi-ch'iu-ching (那先比丘經) Milindapañhā	1670
64	*Ch.* *Skt.*	Ta-ch'eng-chi-p'u-sa-hsüeh-lun (大乘集菩薩學論) Śikṣāsamuccaya	1636
65	*Ch.*	Shih-mo-ho-yen-lun (釋摩訶衍論)	1688
66-I	*Ch.* *Eng.*	Pan-jo-po-lo-mi-to-hsin-ching-yu-tsan (般若波羅蜜多心經幽賛) A Comprehensive Commentary on the Heart Sutra (Prajñāpāramitā-hṛdaya-sūtra)	1710
66-II	*Ch.*	Kuan-wu-liang-shou-fo-ching-shu (觀無量壽佛經疏)	1753
66-III	*Ch.*	San-lun-hsüan-i (三論玄義)	1852

Vol. No.		Title	T. No.
66-IV	*Ch.*	Chao-lun （肇論）	1858
67, 68	*Ch.*	Miao-fa-lien-hua-ching-hsüan-i （妙法蓮華經玄義）	1716
69	*Ch.*	Ta-ch'eng-hsüan-lun （大乘玄論）	1853
70-I	*Ch.*	Hua-yen-i-ch'eng-chiao-i-fên-ch'i-chang （華嚴一乘教義分齊章）	1866
70-II	*Ch.*	Yüan-jên-lun （原人論）	1886
70-III	*Ch.*	Hsiu-hsi-chih-kuan-tso-ch'an-fa-yao （修習止觀坐禪法要）	1915
70-IV	*Ch.*	T'ien-t'ai-ssŭ-chiao-i （天台四教儀）	1931
71, 72	*Ch.*	Mo-ho-chih-kuan （摩訶止觀）	1911
73-I	*Ch.*	Kuo-ch'ing-pai-lu （國清百録）	1934
73-II	*Ch.*	Liu-tsu-ta-shih-fa-pao-t'an-ching （六祖大師法寶壇經）	2008
	Eng.	The Platform Sutra of the Sixth Patriarch	
73-III	*Ch.*	Huang-po-shan-tuan-chi-ch'an-shih-ch'uan-hsin-fa-yao （黄檗山斷際禪師傳心法要）	2012A
73-IV	*Ch.*	Yung-chia-chêng-tao-ko （永嘉證道歌）	2014
74-I	*Ch.*	Chên-chou-lin-chi-hui-chao-ch'an-shih-wu-lu （鎭州臨濟慧照禪師語録）	1985
	Eng.	The Recorded Sayings of Linji (In Three Chan Classics)	
74-II	*Ch.*	Wu-mên-kuan （無門關）	2005
	Eng.	Wumen's Gate (In Three Chan Classics)	
74-III	*Ch.*	Hsin-hsin-ming （信心銘）	2010
	Eng.	The Faith-Mind Maxim (In Three Chan Classics)	
74-IV	*Ch.*	Ch'ih-hsiu-pai-chang-ch'ing-kuei （勅修百丈清規）	2025

Vol. No.		Title	T. No.
75	*Ch.*	Fo-kuo-yüan-wu-ch'an-shih-pi-yen-lu (佛果圜悟禪師碧巖録)	2003
	Eng.	The Blue Cliff Record	
76-I	*Ch.*	I-pu-tsung-lun-lun (異部宗輪論)	2031
	Skt.	Samayabhedoparacanacakra	
76-II	*Ch.*	A-yü-wang-ching (阿育王經)	2043
	Skt.	Aśokarāja-sūtra (?)	
	Eng.	The Biographical Scripture of King Aśoka	
76-III	*Ch.*	Ma-ming-p'u-sa-ch'uan (馬鳴菩薩傳)	2046
	Eng.	The Life of Aśvaghoṣa Bodhisattva (In Lives of Great Monks and Nuns)	
76-IV	*Ch.*	Lung-shu-p'u-sa-ch'uan (龍樹菩薩傳)	2047
	Eng.	The Life of Nāgārjuna Bodhisattva (In Lives of Great Monks and Nuns)	
76-V	*Ch.*	P'o-sou-p'an-tou-fa-shih-ch'uan (婆藪槃豆法師傳)	2049
	Eng.	Biography of Dharma Master Vasubandhu (In Lives of Great Monks and Nuns)	
76-VI	*Ch.*	Pi-ch'iu-ni-ch'uan (比丘尼傳)	2063
	Eng.	Biographies of Buddhist Nuns (In Lives of Great Monks and Nuns)	
76-VII	*Ch.*	Kao-sêng-fa-hsien-ch'uan (高僧法顯傳)	2085
	Eng.	The Journey of the Eminent Monk Faxian (In Lives of Great Monks and Nuns)	
76-VIII	*Ch.*	Yu-fang-chi-ch'ao: T'ang-ta-ho-shang-tung-chêng-ch'uan (遊方記抄: 唐大和上東征傳)	2089-(7)
77	*Ch.*	Ta-t'ang-ta-tz'ŭ-ên-ssŭ-san-ts'ang-fa-shih-ch'uan (大唐大慈恩寺三藏法師傳)	2053
	Eng.	A Biography of the Tripiṭaka Master of the Great Ci'en Monastery of the Great Tang Dynasty	
78	*Ch.*	Kao-sêng-ch'uan (高僧傳)	2059
79	*Ch.*	Ta-t'ang-hsi-yü-chi (大唐西域記)	2087
	Eng.	The Great Tang Dynasty Record of the Western Regions	

Vol. No.		Title	T. No.
80	*Ch.*	Hung-ming-chi (弘明集)	2102
81–92	*Ch.*	Fa-yüan-chu-lin (法苑珠林)	2122
93-I	*Ch.*	Nan-hai-chi-kuei-nei-fa-ch'uan (南海寄歸内法傳)	2125
	Eng.	Buddhist Monastic Traditions of Southern Asia	
93-II	*Ch.*	Fan-yü-tsa-ming (梵語雑名)	2135
94-I	*Jp.*	Shō-man-gyō-gi-sho (勝鬘經義疏)	2185
94-II	*Jp.*	Yui-ma-kyō-gi-sho (維摩經義疏)	2186
95	*Jp.*	Hok-ke-gi-sho (法華義疏)	2187
96-I	*Jp.*	Han-nya-shin-gyō-hi-ken (般若心經秘鍵)	2203
96-II	*Jp.*	Dai-jō-hos-sō-ken-jin-shō (大乘法相研神章)	2309
96-III	*Jp.*	Kan-jin-kaku-mu-shō (觀心覺夢鈔)	2312
97-I	*Jp.*	Ris-shū-kō-yō (律宗綱要)	2348
	Eng.	The Essentials of the Vinaya Tradition	
97-II	*Jp.*	Ten-dai-hok-ke-shū-gi-shū (天台法華宗義集)	2366
	Eng.	The Collected Teachings of the Tendai Lotus School	
97-III	*Jp.*	Ken-kai-ron (顯戒論)	2376
97-IV	*Jp.*	San-ge-gaku-shō-shiki (山家學生式)	2377
98-I	*Jp.*	Hi-zō-hō-yaku (秘藏寶鑰)	2426
98-II	*Jp.*	Ben-ken-mitsu-ni-kyō-ron (辨顯密二教論)	2427
98-III	*Jp.*	Soku-shin-jō-butsu-gi (即身成佛義)	2428
98-IV	*Jp.*	Shō-ji-jis-sō-gi (聲字實相義)	2429
98-V	*Jp.*	Un-ji-gi (吽字義)	2430
98-VI	*Jp.*	Go-rin-ku-ji-myō-hi-mitsu-shaku (五輪九字明秘密釋)	2514

Vol. No.		Title	*T.* No.
98-VII	*Jp.*	Mitsu-gon-in-hotsu-ro-san-ge-mon (密嚴院發露懺悔文)	2527
98-VIII	*Jp.*	Kō-zen-go-koku-ron (興禪護國論)	2543
98-IX	*Jp.*	Fu-kan-za-zen-gi (普勧坐禪儀)	2580
99–103	*Jp.*	Shō-bō-gen-zō (正法眼藏)	2582
104-I	*Jp.*	Za-zen-yō-jin-ki (坐禪用心記)	2586
104-II	*Jp.*	Sen-chaku-hon-gan-nen-butsu-shū (選擇本願念佛集)	2608
	Eng.	Senchaku Hongan Nembutsu Shū	
104-III	*Jp.*	Ris-shō-an-koku-ron (立正安國論)	2688
	Eng.	Risshōankokuron or The Treatise on the Establishment of the Orthodox Teaching and the Peace of the Nation (In Two Nichiren Texts)	
104-IV	*Jp.*	Kai-moku-shō (開目抄)	2689
	Eng.	Kaimokushō or Liberation from Blindness	
104-V	*Jp.*	Kan-jin-hon-zon-shō (觀心本尊抄)	2692
	Eng.	Kanjinhonzonsho or The Most Venerable One Revealed by Introspecting Our Minds for the First Time at the Beginning of the Fifth of the Five Five Hundred-year Ages (In Two Nichiren Texts)	
104-VI	*Ch.*	Fu-mu-ên-chung-ching (父母恩重經)	2887
105-I	*Jp.*	Ken-jō-do-shin-jitsu-kyō-gyō-shō-mon-rui (顯淨土眞實教行証文類)	2646
105-II	*Jp.*	Tan-ni-shō (歎異抄)	2661
	Eng.	Tannishō: Passages Deploring Deviations of Faith	
106-I	*Jp.*	Ren-nyo-shō-nin-o-fumi (蓮如上人御文)	2668
	Eng.	Rennyo Shōnin Ofumi: The Letters of Rennyo	
106-II	*Jp.*	Ō-jō-yō-shū (往生要集)	2682
107-I	*Jp.*	Has-shū-kō-yō (八宗綱要)	蔵外
	Eng.	The Essentials of the Eight Traditions	

Vol. No.		Title	T. No.
107-II	*Jp.*	San-gō-shī-ki （三教指帰）	蔵外
107-III	*Jp.*	Map-pō-tō-myō-ki （末法燈明記）	蔵外
	Eng.	The Candle of the Latter Dharma	
107-IV	*Jp.*	Jū-shichi-jō-ken-pō （十七條憲法）	蔵外